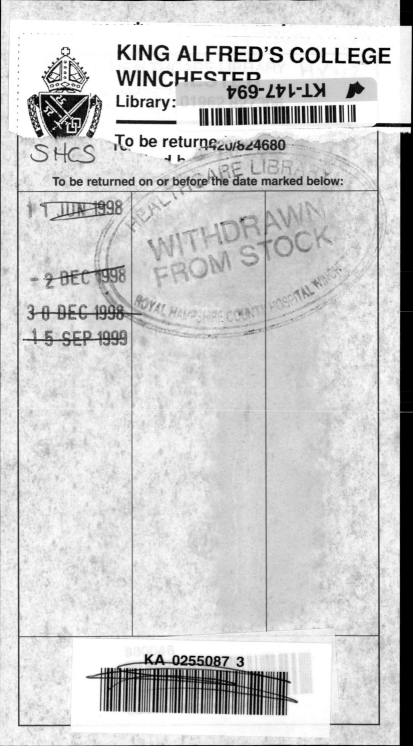

COUNSELLING FOR WOMEN

· COUNSELLING IN CONTEXT ·

Series editors
Moira Walker and Michael Jacobs
University of Leicester

Counselling takes place in many different contexts: in voluntary and statutory agencies; in individual private practice or in a consortium; at work, in medical settings, in churches and in different areas of education. While there may be much in common in basic counselling methods (despite theoretical differences), each setting gives rise to particular areas of concern, and often requires specialist knowledge, both of the problems likely to be brought, but also of the context in which the client is being seen. Even common counselling issues vary slightly from situation to situation in the way they are applied and understood.

This series examines eleven such areas, and applies a similar scheme to each, first looking at the history of the development of counselling in the particular context; then at the context itself, and how the counsellor fits into it. Central to each volume are chapters on common issues related to the specific setting and questions that may be peculiar to it but could be of interest and value to counsellors working elsewhere. Each book will provide useful information for anyone considering counselling, or the provision of counselling in a particular context. Relationships with others who work in the same setting whether as counsellors, managers or administrators are also examined; and each book concludes with the author's own critique of counselling as it is currently practised in that context.

Current and forthcoming titles

COUNSELLING FOR WOMEN

Janet Perry

OPEN UNIVERSITY PRESS
Buckingham · Philadelphia

Open University Press
Celtic Court
22 Ballmoor
Buckingham
MK18 1XW

and

1900 Frost Road, Suite 101
Bristol, PA 19007, USA

First Published 1993

A catalogue record of this book is available from the British Library

ISBN 0 335 19034 0 (pb)

Library of Congress Cataloging-in-Publication Data
Perry, Janet, 1947–
Counselling for women / by Janet Perry.
p.   cm.—(Counselling in context)
Includes bibliographical references (p.   ) and index.
ISBN 0–335–19034–0 (pb)
1. Women—Counselling of—Great Britain.   2. Feminist therapy—
Great Britain.   I. Title.   II. Series.
HV1448.G7P47   1993
362.83'86'0941—dc20
93–15402   CIP

Typeset by Graphicraft Typesetters Ltd, Hong Kong
Printed in Great Britain by St Edmundsbury Press Ltd,
Bury St Edmunds, Suffolk

To Frances, Joss and Rachel

Contents

Series editors' preface

In this volume the role of women in counselling is explored in the context of different organizations, illustrating the range of counselling activities undertaken by women from the formal to the informal, and demonstrating the flexibility and creativity required to respond effectively to the needs of women. Their role as carers is examined, in terms of the opportunities it creates, whilst also acknowledging and discussing the potential and actual dilemmas of this role.

It is no accident that this volume on Counselling in Women's Organizations is one of the first in this series. Women have been marginalized for too long, and it is our concern in producing this series that organizations that represent their needs are in the forefront. It is now widely recognized that traditional mental health services have generally failed to match their service provision to the needs of women. Indeed, in many instances questions relating to need have not even been addressed, let alone resulted in positive developments and changes. It is a worrying fact that women are far greater users of all mental health services than men; and yet the complex and interweaving psychological, social and political reasons for this, are rarely taken seriously or reflected in women's treatment.

Throughout history women have been the carers of others; a role that whilst thrust on them, is also valued by them, although not always so by a wider society. We live in strongly patriarchal and capitalistic times, and although lip service is paid to caring, this is not reflected in adequate resourcing and effective policies. In this volume Janet Perry shows how services for women can all too easily be demolished in a harsh economic climate, and how frequently they are first in the firing line of vicious spending cuts. Lip service and political cant come cheap; translating this into action is expensive.

In recent years women's traditional role of caring for others has taken a new direction. Many women have turned to counselling, both as a way of receiving help that is seen as more women centred than other helping approaches, and as a way of offering care and help to other women. Most students on most counselling courses are women; most volunteer counsellors are women. Similar to all other professions, as the career ladder is mounted more men are represented, but even so counselling is a field where women occupy a growing and significant role. As Janet Perry clearly demonstrates the growth of counselling, and the greater use of counselling skills, have opened doors for women that they have entered with great enthusiasm and skill. As she also shows it is a sad indictment of modern times that many of these newly created opportunities are now under threat. Once again, it seems, women are expendable, and they suffer the effects of political expedience, as they have so often done throughout history.

Moira Walker
Michael Jacobs

Acknowledgements

I am left with two very strong feelings having written this book. One is of enormous respect and admiration for the women clients and counsellors associated with the organizations I have been researching. So much has been achieved and learnt by them in a short space of time. The other feeling is one of gloom and foreboding. Will there be a future for these organizations in the present economic climate? The first feeling will stay with me: I hope my pessimism is unfounded.

Many thanks are due for the help and encouragement given to me. Very special thanks to Pam Goddard and Helen Lawson of Boston Women's Aid, Marion Bennett of Derby Rape Crisis, Peggy Sinclair of Leicester Home-Start, Gill Martin and Lesley Clements of Leeds Women's Therapy Centre, Margy Wallis of Pen Green Family Centre, Panna Modi of Leicester Family Service Unit, and also to Moira Walker for her supportive and stimulating editing. Finally I want to thank my family for their tolerance and enthusiasm; my mother for her unfailing interest in both the material and the progress of the work; and my husband Richard Wood for his gentle support as well as for typing the manuscript.

· ONE ·

The development of counselling in women's organizations

Throughout history women have joined together to help other women in all aspects of their lives. In earlier times this inevitably focused on family and domestic lives, and while this is still the case it has now extended to professional and political areas. This long history of coming together for mutual support has been both formal and informal. Women have offered services to other women appropriate to their needs and although these helpers cannot always have shared the same experience as those they help, they have in common the experience of being in a society which discriminates against them.

Women operate in a variety of organizations, some founded to serve directly the purposes of male philanthropists or women's professional bodies, while some have originated from women moved by the plight of other women. If long established, they often reflect both the social issues of the time in which initially they developed and the original reasons which gave rise to their existence. Those of more recent origin reflect contemporary social issues and the experience of women in society today. The organizational model might be one borrowed from among those developed by men but uniquely adapted to serve the purposes of women, or it might be a model that asserts that different, usually non-hierarchical structures are required for women.

HISTORICAL CONTEXT

Historically, women's organizations have enabled women to have an arena of their own in which to express themselves, be of service

to others, and be responsible for their own organizations and sometimes, even, for their own lives. The earliest example is that of
women's religious orders. Women were, as now, marginalized by
early Orthodox and Catholic Christianity although, interestingly, the
Celtic tradition of Christianity, with its emphasis on the necessity of
being in tune with the earth and of the importance of female cycles,
patterns and rhythms was a significant exception. However, to be
a woman member of a religious order during the Middle Ages meant
that a woman was submitting her life to the rule of other women
rather than to the rule of men, as was the case in the world outside.
Furthermore, the woman who was Head of the Order could be an
influential, highly respected, powerful person in her own right. She
might, for instance, travel widely and independently and be asked
to give advice and counsel to rulers and popes (Bowie and Davies
1990: 7). In time, the women's sections of the Protestant and
Nonconformist churches often offered women more power and influence than was available elsewhere within contemporary society
(Braithwaite 1961: 270–1).

Similarly, women's educational institutions offered the opportunity for girls and women to develop educationally in their own
way, although these arose from a range of motivations. For instance,
Cheltenham Ladies College was founded in 1853 by a group of men
to train each girl sufficiently to 'fit her for the discharge of those
duties which devolve upon her as a wife, mother, mistress and
friend', but without undermining their superior position (Holdsworth
1988: 41). Or they could arise from an apparently benevolent,
although patronizing, desire to protect women. Whatever the reason, women educationalists, such as Dorothea Beale, second principal
of Cheltenham Ladies College who 'opposed the received wisdom
of the time with vigour and passion' (Holdsworth 1988: 41), were
determined in their efforts to provide quality education for their
students. Interestingly, only fifty years on, at the beginning of the
twentieth century, the providers of community adult education were
concerned that women took advantage of their services. The Workers
Educational Association, established in 1903, was primarily concerned
at that time with the educationally underprivileged, and in its early
days it paid particular attention to the needs of women. Leaflets
published in 1912 described its positive discrimination in favour of
women (Hughes and Kennedy 1985: 114). Historically, this desire
to provide educational opportunities for women has been an important strand in the development of community adult education.

With the admission of women to the professions at the beginning
of this century, it was a significant step forward when women's

educational institutions could be staffed by women teachers. At the same time there also arose the possibility that women's health projects could be staffed by women nurses and doctors. This question of women caring for women, particularly in gender-specific health areas, is still a hotly debated issue. There is a clear need and demand for well-women clinics and family planning clinics to be staffed by women. Women's health issues must be taken more seriously and the health services response should be sensitive to women's feelings. An example of good practice are the innovatory breast screening clinics in some general hospitals, staffed entirely by women, including most importantly, women surgeons and women consultants.

Women's organizations have usually come into being to address one aspect of women's lives. Frequently they have evolved from a particular social concern. The Women's Institute, for instance, grew out of a social concern during The Great War about the state of the nation's health and nutritional standards at the time, combined with a feeling that women should be encouraged to be 'good housekeepers' (Holdsworth 1988: 19). As an organization the Women's Institute so effectively upholds the dignity of women and of traditional female skills and crafts that it effectively challenges and demolishes the original reason for its existence, namely that women were inadequate housekeepers.

Women have been active politically both within community action (Wallis 1992: 23) and the political parties since before the beginning of the twentieth century, although they are still grossly underrepresented in Parliament – in the 1992 General Election only 60 out of 651 MPs elected were women. The women's groups that arose in the 1980s in response to particular issues of the time, for example women supporting the miners strike, and women at Greenham Common, spotlighted and gave credence to their abilities to organize, manage and sustain their own political action. A significant consequence of being involved in political action was that women discovered how much they changed, both personally and in terms of their relationships, particularly within their families. They recognized that women's political action groups are empowering. They became a vehicle for change and personal growth of their members in the same way as counselling and therapy can be.

Many organizations have evolved from a growing awareness and realization of the appalling quality of some women's lives, brought to light by the Women's Movement over the last few decades. Rape Crisis Centres, Women's Aid Hostels, as well as specialist projects for women survivors of childhood abuse, remind us of the unacceptable violence many women are subject to. Such organizations were founded by women in response to the suffering in other women's lives. In addition, they were established because of the inadequate response of the statutory and public services, which frequently discount and marginalize women's experiences. Those responsible for founding these groups may or may not have been subject to the same violence as the women who use them.

Culture-specific projects, such as Asian Women's Centres and Chinese Women's Counselling Projects, have developed from within those communities. They grow from a recognition that issues facing women from different cultures in this country are the same, but also different, from those facing other women. They are similar in that all women encounter a core of common issues, but different in that beyond this core, crucial and powerful cultural differences exist regarding the perception and treatment of women. Such projects also recognize the effects of both sexism and racism in women's lives.

Other groups are concerned with women as mothers. Projects set up for parents and families are very often regarded as women's organizations. Home-Start is an example, providing a befriending service for parents of under school age children. While the service was set up to work with both parents, the vast majority of its volunteers are women who work mostly with mothers of young children. In the same way, Family Centres and the voluntary Social Work agency, Family Service Units, work with many more mothers than fathers. In reality parenting becomes gender-specific: it is the mother who becomes identified as the parent. In both these settings women's groups and specialist facilities are provided for women. These may include women's health groups, the provision of health services, and the opportunity of adult education classes, including Open University courses run by women staff members. Access to education is seen as vital in some centres recognizing that women's educational careers are different from their male counterparts, particularly for working class women. This may reflect a belief that education, for many women, is one route out from unsatisfactory lives.

COUNSELLING WITHIN WOMEN'S ORGANIZATIONS

Women's organizations are many and varied: those above can only serve as illustrations of this range. Within this, some are set up to provide a counselling service to women, some having the provision of a therapy and counselling service for women as a primary function, whilst others include counselling or supportive listening as one among many purposes. Most work with women individually and in groups. The significance of working with women in groups will be explored later in this chapter.

In exploring counselling in the context of women's projects, I find it useful to identify the different ways in which the counselling function is expressed. First, there are Women's Therapy and Counselling Centres which specialize in therapeutic services to women. Second are organizations which provide counselling as one approach among many, and in which the counselling is usually a response to a particular issue. I have also included in this category projects such as Rape Crisis Centres, which provide a counselling service for a specific problem or situation. Third there are those organizations, such as Women's Aid, which make use of counselling skills in both one-to-one and groupwork with women.

Although currently there are only four, Women's Therapy Centres in this country have made a very great contribution to our understanding and thinking about the counselling needs of women and how these should be addressed. The therapeutic services offered by Women's Therapy Centres are counselling, psychotherapy, and therapy groups; some offer all three, some a combination of two. Women's Therapy Centres may also offer their own training courses to women therapists and a variety of workshops open to all women, on topics ranging from depression and abortion to issues aimed specifically at women professionals, such as social workers, solicitors, and health visitors, whose clientele are women. Sometimes the service will be free, sometimes client contributions are encouraged according to ability to pay. The pioneering London Women's Therapy Centre was established in 1976 and has provided a model for the centres established since, in Birmingham, Leeds and Sheffield. Writers from the Women's Therapy Centres have influenced thinking about the issues women bring to therapy and of providing services congruent to the needs of women users.

In the second category are those organizations in which counselling takes place as one response amongst others, or as a response to a specific problem or circumstance. When counselling is the main aim, its provision is less problematic than when it is one of a number of services. In specialist projects, the service can be offered and organized in a way which helps rather than hinders the process. The style of organization will also reflect the belief system of the particular agency relating to the problems or situations it encounters. A Rape Crisis Centre, for example, will be organized around its

main aim, the provision of counselling, but also strongly demonstrates its belief that rape is an extreme example of the abuse of
male power.

In women's organizations where counselling takes place alongside other activities, providing a context in which this can take
place becomes more complicated, as a range of services has to be
incorporated and catered for. Sometimes women's counselling projects exist within structures which also provide help for men and
children, so making the situation even more complex. An example
is the service provided in Family Centres, where the major aim is
to provide nursery care for children.

In the last category are those groups which make use of counselling skills. They are very clear that the workers and volunteers
employing these skills are not counsellors, although workers will
undertake some training in appropriate skills in order to offer users
a befriending or supportive listening service. These will be used to
enable them to work in one-to-one situations with women as well
as with groups. Additionally the women trainers will model ways of
working with women in their teaching.

Development of counselling within women's organizations

Counselling has developed widely since the 1970s, and nowadays
many more people are employed as counsellors, in a paid or voluntary capacity, whilst others use counselling skills in their work
(Dryden *et al*. 1989: xiii). Even more people are students on counselling courses, and it is to the advantage of women's organizations who recruit counsellors, that the majority of students on such
courses are women.

In projects which were initiated to address a particular aspect
of women's lives, an understanding developed of how issues are
inevitably interlinked, and a desire arose therefrom to respond
to women as 'whole people'. The value system which underlies
counselling and counselling skills allows such a response to take
place. Attentive listening, acceptance, warmth, and a belief in a
person's innate goodness and potential for growth are a prerequisite
for responding to a woman. The desire to respond to the 'whole
woman' came from a wish to move away from relating to her as
someone only defined in relation to others, so valuing her essentially in her own right, and for her own self. Relating to women as
if they were merely a collection of roles centred on serving others,
for example as mother, wife, etc., has been a major consequence of

their considerable disadvantage and position in our society. This has led to a feeling of invisiblity, as if a complete and whole existence is not for them.

Entering counselling will often be the first time a woman has ever been given guaranteed time and space consistently, where she is granted confidentiality accompanied by a non-judgemental, accepting attitude within a potentially close relationship. Particularly for those subject to abuse in childhood or violence in adult relationships it is likely to be a unique experience of being treated as someone in her own right, with needs, desires and wants of her own, rather than being the object of someone else's exploitation.

Groups working with mothers have realized that it was impossible to support them in this role without addressing their wider needs. The very nature of being a mother means that she has little time for herself and receives little recognition or economic reward. For those who work in this field it is central to their philosophy that supporting women as mothers cannot happen without acknowledging and working with these wider issues. So counselling, while giving time and space to mothers also acknowledges the difficulties of this role and re-enforces its value and meaning.

The interlinking of issues in women's lives became apparent as more was discovered about areas such as depression and abuse of women and children. Both these experiences commonly lead women to seek counselling in order to cope more effectively with their symptoms, causes and effects. Women coming together to provide a supportive service to mothers, such as Home-Start, found that large numbers of those they were working with were either depressed because of other factors or were disclosing some sort of abuse (usually sexual) in childhood.

Not surprisingly Family Centres and groups such as Home-Start identified the need for the provision of services for depressed mothers. The reasons for this are two-fold. First, many more women than men present as depressed, seek help from their GPs and are diagnosed as such. At all ages the rates of depression are higher for women but one group particularly at risk are mothers who stay at home with pre-school age children. Two different studies (Brown and Harris 1978, and Richman 1976: 75–8) have indicated that at least a third of women of three-year old children and pre-school age children are significantly depressed. Additionally, working class women are five times more likely to be depressed than middle class women (Brown and Harris 1978). One response to this situation is to offer individual or group counselling to women who are depressed. It could be argued that this class factor suggests that other measures of a more politically radical nature are needed if this issue is to be seriously addressed.

Second, women prefer to seek counselling in settings they are already connected to and where they feel safe, rather than use psychiatric services which are far more likely to be stigmatizing. Studies show that women have been discriminated against and stereotyped by psychiatric services (Walker 1990: 66) and very often find such services unsympathetic to their needs. Counselling centres which offer a specialized, easily obtainable and accessible service for symptoms of mental discomfort are still few and far between (Oldfield 1983: 7), and so women are likely to ask for counselling help from agencies which are familiar to them.

THE IMPACT OF CHILDHOOD ABUSE ON COUNSELLING WOMEN

The disclosure by increasing numbers of women of some form of abuse in childhood or adulthood has become an issue of major concern for many women's projects and groups. The abuse of women and children was brought to our attention by the work of the Women's Movement during the 1970s and 1980s and was then taken up by the media. When Childline was established in the mid 1980s it was soon found that approximately half the calls received were from adult survivors of abuse seeking counselling for a problem that had been hidden too long. It seems that permission to seek help was given to those adults in a way that had not been triggered, two decades earlier, by the 'discovery' of baby battering, the physical abuse of children (Kempe and Kempe 1978: 17). This tremendous upsurge of women disclosing sexual abuse and subsequently seeking counselling affected many of those working with women by making an aspect of their lives visible that was previously invisible.

The response of some women's organizations to the overwhelming demand for help in this area was the setting up of specialist counselling services (Perry 1992: 46–59). This could exist within an established agency such as a Family Centre, or a different organization could be encouraged and supported in its provision. In the latter case this would very often be a self-help response. Whatever its basis the workers needed training in counselling skills and counselling, and appropriate help and supervision. The details they encountered were so horrific, and affected workers in so many ways, that it reinforced very starkly the need both for good counselling practice and for good supervision. Thus, individual women's tragedies and society's recognition of their existence has also promoted the recognition, acceptance and acknowledgement of professional counselling practice.

Many women's projects, in making a response to disclosure of childhood abuse, decided that a counselling service to women as individuals was not appropriate but that the provision of counselling in groups was. This response was, in part, expedient; there were too many women seeking help for the projects to be able to help on an individual basis. More importantly the response came from a belief in the effectiveness of offering counselling to women in groups. These model, as individual Feminist counselling also does, that women's individual experiences can be seen within a social and political context. Some projects, such as Women's Aid, are clear that they work with women in groups only because of this. They believe that to counsel a woman individually may imply that the counsellor believed that her experiences, for example of being violently treated by men, resulted from individual pathology. Such an implication may be unintended, but could nevertheless be present. Others would feel equally strongly that individual counselling *need* not carry such a message, although they would recognize that it *could*. It can be argued that groups empower people more directly than individual counselling, and that working in groups is a particularly powerful model for working with disadvantaged women (Butler and Wintram 1991: 70). It is also especially relevant when confronting specific issues, for instance enabling the disclosure of secrets and shame relating to abuse and violence. The strength and power of such secrets and their hold over individuals can most effectively be challenged and dispelled using this model.

Although a very powerful case can therefore be made for groupwork with women, a similarly powerful one could be made for individual counselling. Many would argue that what is central is that a real choice is available for each woman in her unique situation. For some, their chosen mode will be individual time, for others it will be participating in a group. Some may not be ready to share their pain and difficulties with more than one other person and it is essential that this choice is not invalidated or pathologized. It is perhaps crucial that the two modes stand side by side, offering a real and significant choice. It would be unfortunate if they competed for superiority. Their dual existance offers a valuable complementarity. They both have a validity and appropriateness of their own.

THE IMPLICATIONS OF THE CHANGING ROLES OF
WOMEN FOR COUNSELLING

Following legislation of the early and mid 1970s, notably The Sex Discrimination Act and The Employment Protection Act, life for women at work has steadily altered, but increased opportunities have also brought increased pressures and new stresses, particularly for working mothers. In the mid 1970s it was still unusual for women to return to work after the birth of a baby. In the 1990s there is a greater social expectation that a new mother will carry on working, although she is still provided with few child care resources to ease her decision. There is an increasing awareness of the stresses and strains for women who have both a family and paid employment outside the home, and have to juggle their different roles of worker, mother, sexual partner, housekeeper, and more. As the working lives of women change so different areas of tension arise. For instance, although the Sex Discrimination Act of 1975 apparently extended the range of jobs available to women, many industries and professions remained male-dominated, and women working in them experienced isolation and discrimination. As women enter managerial positions previously the prerogative of men, they have to contend with isolation and vulnerability. Some of the generation of women who, twenty years ago, joined professions and industries, are now more likely to climb the career ladder. They enter the 'uncharted territory' of women in senior and top management positions. Infiltrating traditional male domains is not always comfortable, particularly for women who challenge established management styles. Women in this position remain a small, although growing, number relative to their male colleagues. However clinical practice indicates an increase in the number of these women in management positions seeking counselling for work issues. Counselling offers time and space for her to work out how to 'be' as a manager, and can validate her right to a management style that is different from that of her male colleagues. It also offers a consistent, nurturing relationship to a woman now responsible for both the smooth running of relationships within her staff team, as well as those at home.

Increasingly support groups are being set up by women in management and in institutions where they are few in number, for example senior staff in higher education or health authorities. They are time limited, closed groups in order to allow for trust and feelings of safety to grow. They incorporate the use of counselling and listening skills and encourage participants to work with one another to dispel feelings of isolation.

THE DEVELOPMENT OF SELF-HELP GROUPS

As I have discussed previously, the development of counselling within women's organizations has been influenced by several factors: the wish to respond to the 'whole' woman rather than to fragments of her life and self; the impact of the numbers requesting counselling following the disclosure of childhood abuse; and the high incidence of depression in women. However another significant strand in the development of counselling has been the establishment of women's self-help groups. The distinction between self-help groups and other services is not always absolute and many organizations discussed in this book are, in some senses, part of the self-help movement.

The founders of self-help groups recognized unmet needs as a result of their own experiences and their own difficulty in locating appropriate help. Thus Home-Start, now a national organization working with volunteers to provide a befriending service to parents of pre-school age children, grew from the experiences of one woman, Margaret Harrison, of being both a parent and a professional worker. Similarly, Cruse, initially set up as a women's organization providing befriending support to widows, grew to help all bereaved people. Self-help groups, such as Abuse Survivors Groups or Anorexic Aid, and organizations such as Women's Aid or Rape Crisis were started in response to the lack of provision by the statutory services. While the latter appeared to recognize violence in women's lives, until very recently the automatic official response remained one of blaming the victim. A further central and essential strand in the development of self-help groups is the belief that the most effective support is given by women who have shared similar experiences.

As these groups encountered complicated and daunting areas of women's lives so grew the recognition of the need for counselling training. Women who facilitated abuse survivors groups undertook training in counselling skills and also recognized a need for an awareness of group dynamics. They arranged consultancy, supervision and training for themselves. Specialist trainers were sought, and links made with counsellors who worked with abuse survivors. Further, it was recognized that facilitators were confronting their own personal issues. Survivors helping other women survivors needed to ensure and maintain very clear boundaries between their own experiences and those of group members. Detailed and sensitive supervision was vital. It was also thought necessary for facilitators to be in therapy themselves, demonstrating the important belief in counselling as appropriate for all women rather than an esoteric service for the few. The women's self-help movement, together with the Women's Therapy Centres, responded to the criticism levelled at counselling and therapy, that it is largely a white, middle class activity (Ernst and Maguire 1987: 8) for the well educated, and have sought to provide a more accessible, more readily available and widespread service.

IMPACT OF COUNSELLING TRAINING

As I noted before, a major factor in the development of counselling in this field has been the growth of counselling courses, and the increasing use of volunteer counsellors. Most students are women, and the majority of volunteer counsellors were and are women. For many, counselling training came at a time when child care needs were not so pressing and where new career directions were being sought. Entering training at this stage in their lives represented for many a period of great 'personal growth' and of 'finding oneself'. The experience of motherhood had highlighted for many the ways in which women, for some including themselves, were disadvantaged and discounted in that role. Counselling training clearly has a tremendous impact on women trainees in terms of their growing assertiveness and feelings of increased self-esteem and value. For many this has been a very significant counterbalance to how, as mothers, their positive feelings were eroded by society's discounting and invalidating of that crucial role. Those who have experienced such change and growth within their own lives can bring optimism, enthusiasm and inspiration to their work as volunteer counsellors. For others it may lead to a career change to full-time counselling. After some years, gaining experience in mostly unpaid counselling, many seek more consistently paid work in salaried posts or through private practice (Dryden et al. 1989: 15). Many had originally trained in other professions, for example as teachers or social workers: professions which at one time had offered women status and respect. These are now professions which have become increasingly demoralized and victimized by the recent emphasis on private enterprise to the detriment of public service. So women professionals, working in education and social services, have become discounted in a way that reflects how women are discounted in society at large.

This raises the interesting question of why counselling as an alternative profession is so attractive. Clearly the value base of counselling is one women are deeply in sympathy with, often the reason for training in their original profession, before effective practice became increasingly difficult as the profession became demoralized. A further reason for its appeal is the emphasis, value and importance placed on intuition and feelings rather than rationality. Jocelyn Chaplin confirms this view when she writes 'at times I have felt that the world of counselling is one of the few areas of modern culture in which the values and thinking associated with the female gender are genuinely respected' (Chaplin 1989: 223).

IMPACT OF COUNSELLING ON ORGANIZATIONAL STRUCTURES

Another significant feature of these developments has been their impact and influence on organizational structures both in terms of their day-to-day running and of the service delivery. For some women's organizations a key philosophy is that their structure should reflect the value base of their work. For instance, a Women's Aid Project might appoint women workers for their personal qualities rather than their qualifications, reflecting their belief that insistence on qualifications is inevitably discriminatory. Additionally workers will be jointly responsible for the project, thereby creating a non-hierarchical structure. In the same way, Women's Therapy Centres may be 'co-ordinated' rather than managed: therapists co-ordinate and are responsible for their own areas of expertise, joining together for business and policy making meetings on an equal basis. Women's Therapy Centres are also aware of the need to explore the significance of their own group dynamics as well as informing themselves of how women work together in all sorts of ways. The acquisition and practice of counselling skills are invaluable when working co-operatively in these ways. This philosophy and practice is radically different from that of traditionally male dominated management and organizational styles.

Home-Start also demonstrates this move away from traditional models. Its use of counselling skills and philosophies extends from the training of volunteer befrienders, and permeates all aspects of the work. They are directly modelled throughout the training, emphasizing the importance of listening, empathizing and validating individuals. Therefore training provides volunteers with a model of 'good parenting' for the families they visit whilst also offering different models of how women can act and be, to volunteers and mothers alike. They demonstrate both the reality and the possibility of women organizing, taking responsibility and being assertive in ways unfamiliar to many.

In Family Centres which emphasize access to educational opportunities for women it has been fascinating to see how using counselling skills as well as being part of the group have become important aspects of the teaching process. The recent recognition that processes of adult learning are very different from those in children's learning has been very significant, with its implication that adult learners have a potential for life-long cognitive growth and development (Wallis 1992: 15). Self-confidence and a sense of control over their own lives are seen as critical factors in adult learning, as are the students' life experiences and insights. Education ceases to be about the imparting of knowledge to the student by the teacher, and becomes a dialogue. 'The tutors method, style and subject become much less important and the students' background, feelings and responses dominate: the peer learning group becomes a powerful force' (Wallis 1992: 17). In this way the tutor's listening skills and the peer group itself become the medium for learning, and is particularly relevant in the case of women students.

WOMEN'S THERAPY CENTRES

The London Women's Therapy Centre has been in operation since 1976 and has served as a model for others which emerged in the 1980s. The London Centre started in the basement of a woman therapist's house and eventually obtained funding from public services and trusts, and space in a building for itself. The founders, and subsequent therapists who worked there, were and are skilled, experienced therapists who perceived a need for a women-only psychotherapy service. There was an understanding that the issues that women bring to counselling and therapy are different because of their social and political position. A clear link was seen between their 'personal' feelings and the political structures in which they live. Issues previously identified as individual problems, for instance feeling powerless or depressed or feeling overwhelmed by others' demands, were seen as common problems shared by many women. They were not the result of individual failure, but arose from the contradictory demands society makes on all women (Ernst and Goodison 1981: 3). Problems which brought women into therapy, for example eating disorders, were increasingly understood in terms of their experience within the family and wider society. Compulsive eating, anorexia, and bulimia were perceived as a complex reaction to a woman's feelings of lack of power and control over her own destiny. The active recognition that women spend an enormous amount of physical and emotional energy looking after other people both within their families and often in paid employment was also significant in their work. They recognized that mothers constantly give out and feed others. Everyone else's needs take precedence over her own, and it is therefore not surprising that feelings of merging with others, feeding others emotionally, not knowing how to take space for themselves, are frequent themes (Orbach 1978: 24). This emphasis on other people's needs and the difficulty of ensuring her own are met can lead to confusion regarding her own bodily needs. Eating can be a way of giving and looking after herself. Overeating can be an attempt to meet some of her own needs; literally to build herself up for the demands made on her. And so it is that fat becomes a Feminist issue. Although nowadays these ideas may be familiar to many readers, they represented a radical move away from traditional views and treatment, and their importance should not be underestimated. This challenge to male-dominated theories which failed to take into account the place of the political and social in the psychology of women marked a major shift in thinking. A therapeutic approach relevant to women's experiences at last came into being.

Links were made between a woman's feelings and symptoms and her status as a 'second class citizen' (Ernst and Maguire 1987: 9), which must be acknowledged and worked out in therapy. The need for a women-only service also came from a concern about the accessibility of that service and the ways in which it should operate and be offered. It was considered essential that counselling and therapy should not remain a white middle class service only for those deemed educated and intelligent enough to be able to use it. For a service to be more accessible to women, its physical environment should be welcoming, inviting, nurturing and not intimidating. Just as different issues are brought by women to therapy, so these also vary according to class and race. Therapy is seen to be helpful and relevant to women from all classes and from all racial backgrounds. Again the environment should take care not to be alienating, but appropriate for all, including lesbian women and those who are disabled. The structure of the organization and the way women therapists related to each other and worked together was of great importance. The writing from the London Women's Therapy Centre has also concentrated on organizational issues and has explored the experience of working in such a structure and its

implications more generally for women's relationships. This strand
of exploration has been a highly significant development, in addition to their work on therapy and related theory. In this way the
philosophy of the whole woman, so pivotal in the growth of the
women's therapy service is reflected both in the writing and thinking as well as in its careful creation of a user-friendly physical environment. This takes me into a discussion of Feminist therapy.

FEMINIST THERAPY

At the present time, Feminist therapists vary in their styles of therapy and the ways in which Feminist ideologies are applied to their
therapeutic work. Some work within a psychodynamic framework,
some in a humanistic way, others in a behavioural/cognitive way.
Increasingly some stress a spiritual dimension to their approach,
taking images, symbols and patterns from ancient female wisdom,
often with pre-Christian imagery.

During the development of the most recent Women's Movement,
from the late 1960s onward, many new Feminist writers questioned
and rejected certain aspects of psychoanalysis. They argued that it
was more concerned to socialize women into their roles as wives
and mothers than to encourage them to take control of their own
lives (Chaplin 1988a: 41). The 1950s and 1960s saw a growth in the
humanistic therapies, partly in reaction to the perceived elitism of
psychoanalysis. Many Feminists were attracted to work human-
istically. During the 1970s, Feminist psychologists studied the early
development of girl-children in a sexist society and other writers
showed how women's second-class status affected their deepest
feelings about themselves (Chodorow 1978: 10).

In Britain during the 1970s, the feeling grew among some women
therapists that humanistic methods did not go deep enough. Little
girls take on their gender identity and thereby their status as second
class citizens very early on in their lives (Ernst and Goodison 1981:
4). Some writers and therapists recognized the need to address unconscious factors linked to women's oppression, whilst also incorporating a political stance and understanding. There was a return to
the study of psychoanalysis and the psychodynamic therapies, which
were examined anew in the light of Feminist ideas (Mitchell 1975:
xv). The setting up of the London Women's Therapy Centre in
1976 was most influential in the development of these ideas and of
Feminist therapy in Britain. Therapists working there used a psychodynamic framework based on these developments but it also

became the place where the different strands of Feminist therapy could interact.

There is no unified, organized school of Feminist therapy, and its techniques cannot be taught. It lies within the attitude and way of relating of the individual therapist. Moira Walker suggests that:

> It reflects, rather, a way of being, believing and understanding. In this way it is a perspective, not a technique, that arises from many sources that flow into and feed one another. It is essentially a perspective that allows fluidity, acknowledges interconnectedness and encourages exploration.
>
> (Walker 1990: 73)

Feminist therapy recognizes the interconnectedness of the inner psychological and the outer social and political worlds. It is aware that women's inner psychologies are deeply affected by their position in society and society's demands that they fulfil specific and often undervalued roles. It is aware that power relationships also exist within therapy. For some this means attempting to equalize the relationship whilst others recognize and acknowledge some degree of hierarchy, see it as inevitable but ensure that it is examined and explored. Working and organizing in a non-hierarchical way has been a vital strand of Feminist therapy. Although many women's organizations which incorporate counselling would not see themselves as practising Feminist therapy, they may nevertheless have been influenced by both the debate and the ideas. Thus their practice, values and philosophy can be profoundly informed and influenced by the ideas and structures of Feminist counselling and Feminist groupwork.

· TWO ·

Counselling in women's organizations

In a general sense, women's organizations are set up and exist to address particular aspects of women's lives. There are many which emphasize a women's role as mother, homemaker and carer, ranging from the National Association of Carers, to Home-Start and the Mothers Union. Women in business and education have their own organizations as do women who are both workers in and consumers of health care services. As I described in Chapter 1, as more was understood about the unequal position of women in society, those organizations such as Rape Crisis and Women's Aid developed to respond to the consequences of inequality, whilst others set up specifically for women sometimes developed into a more general service. As I noted, Cruse (Dryden *et al.* 1989: 7) was originally set up to provide a service for widows, who were a much neglected section of society, but has now developed into a general professional counselling service for the bereaved.

In this chapter I describe in more detail the women's organizations which are the main focus of this book, and which I have referred to in Chapter 1. I start by exploring counselling in the context of Women's Aid and Rape Crisis, two organizations responding to violence in women's lives, and continue by examining Home-Start and Family Centres which both emphasize women's role as mother. Specialist Counselling Projects for women survivors of childhood abuse in Family Centres and Family Service Units are then discussed, and finally I look in more detail at Women's Therapy and Counselling Centres. Although many others could have been included, I chose these projects as they reflect a range of approaches to counselling. They have in common a history of having positively chosen the particular type of counselling intervention, believing in its appropriateness in achieving their organizational aims. These counselling approaches range from the sophisticated use of counselling skills by befrienders and group leaders, for example Women's Aid and Home-Start to the provision of long term women's counselling or therapy services. Some offer a specialist counselling response to a particular problem such as the effects of violence, whereas others, notably Women's Therapy Centres, provide therapeutic services to all women who seek them regardless of the presenting problem. These organizations also reflect a range of theoretical approaches, from the psychodynamic framework of Women's Therapy Centres to the eclectic approaches of other projects.

WOMEN'S AID

Violence, whether it be domestic violence, rape, or the sexual and physical abuse experienced as children, is a feature of many women's lives. Domestic violence towards women has a long history. Traditionally, the law has upheld a man's right to control his wife, by force if necessary. In British law, men had a right to beat their wives until the late nineteenth century (Walker 1990: 153–63). Not until as late as 1976 and the Domestic Violence Act of that year, were women enabled to exclude a violent partner from their homes (Holdsworth 1988: 157). From the early 1970s there was a renewed interest in 'wife-battering', as the emergence of the fast developing Women's Movement was alerting public attention to widespread violence to women in their own homes.

The campaigning of women such as Erin Pizzey raised consciousness about domestic violence and the lack of any response to the problem by the statutory agencies. It led to the establishment of the Chiswick Rescue Centre which offered a safe house to women and children escaping from violent partners. Women's Aid Refuges were set up a few years later. Although an entirely different organization, and completely separate from the Chiswick Centre, they both represented a voluntary rather than a statutory response to domestic violence. By 1975, thirty five local groups had founded the Women's Aid Federation England (WAFE), and established a network of refuges in order to promote the interests of Women's Aid at a national level.

Experience within Women's Aid confirmed the belief that the widespread occurrence of domestic violence was a result of social rather than personal factors (Scottish Women's Aid 1991: 1), being a feature of *all* patriarchal countries and cultures of the world and occurring across *all* social classes. Thus domestic violence was seen, not as the symptom of a 'sick' relationship, but rather as the inevitable outcome of the abuse of the power structure within male–female relationships. Giving consumers of Women's Aid an insight into the wider social aspects of male violence was, and is, seen as an essential feature of the work.

Within the UK there are national organizations to which Women's Aid groups affiliate. WAFE, Scottish Women's Aid, Welsh Women's Aid, and the Northern Ireland organization are all separately funded and act independently (*What is Women's Aid?* 1992). Individual local groups meet on a regional basis to exchange ideas relevant to the locality. Women's Aid groups and refuges are run collectively. Considerable support is given from the national organization on a regional basis to groups and individuals, recognizing that for many women it will be their first experience of working collectively.

Refuges vary in size and type as most groups are unable to choose the type of accommodation for their safe houses. Some are given a small old house, possibly in need of repair, by a local authority. Some rent accommodation from other agencies; some groups may squat when a local authority refuses assistance. Additionally the setting up of separate refuges to meet the needs of specific groups of women where beneficial, for example on the grounds of language or religious belief, is supported. The WAFE logo, incorporating images of young and old and women from various cultures, makes clear their aim to be non-discriminatory. Some refuges employ paid workers, some work with volunteer workers. However they all have in common that they are women-only groups and organizations.

Refuges provide a safe place for women and their children escaping from violent partners. They offer practical and emotional support to women and ensure a 'breathing space' enabling women to make decisions and choices in an informed way about their future. Very often there will be two safe houses run by any one group. The first is for women in crisis, and they will only move on to the second-stage house when they have made a decision that they will not be returning to their homes and partners. They will wait there to be rehoused.

Counselling skills in Women's Aid

Women's Aid workers are clear that although they may be trained in the use of counselling skills, they are not counsellors. There is a reluctance to use the word counsellor since this implies the existence of a 'client', whom they believe has less status in the counselling relationship. Women's Aid workers state that they do not want a woman who is trying to escape the controlling influence of a man, to exchange one form of control for another, perceived in this instance as counselling (Scottish Women's Aid 1991: 2). The concept of a 'client' is unacceptable to them: the aim of workers is to shift the balance of power to the woman and they feel that a counselling model does not do this. However it is felt that by the extensive use of empathy skills a worker can form a more equal relationship with the abused woman.

Women who are treated violently by their partners are very often also sexually and emotionally abused. Once the physical abuse has started a common pattern is that it increases in frequency and severity. For the abused, it leads to feelings of degradation, self-loss, demoralization and worthlessness. In addition, women escaping to refuges are usually in a state of shock. A particularly violent incident might well have precipitated the woman into leaving and seeking outside help. She will show signs and symptoms of being subject to trauma: she may well exhibit symptoms of post-traumatic stress syndrome (Wyatt and Powell 1988: 91–6). When she arrives at the refuge she may need to recount in detail the violent incidents and to keep repeating these accounts. This essential ventilation process is facilitated by the worker's use of counselling skills and her accepting and non-judgemental attitude allows the woman to recount her story in an uninhibited way. Remarks that could be construed as non-accepting would block the woman from talking: most of the outside world either does not believe her story or makes judgements about whether or not she should stay with her partner. She is likely to anticipate judgemental attitudes and it will take her time to accept that a Women's Aid worker can behave differently.

Once this initial stage has passed, the worker's aim is to enable the woman to talk about her problems, and to help her recognize herself as abused. Increased awareness of her options will enable her to make decisions about her future. None of this can happen until the woman trusts the worker; not an easy task in the circumstances. She will have been told repeatedly that she caused the violence, and therefore she probably believes that it was her fault or that she deserved it. Although she will be encouraged to talk through her situation and her feelings, this will not happen in any formal sense. The talking will happen spontaneously as she wishes and as it arises. It will inevitably compete with other demands; phone calls and the needs of other women residents and their children. It is likely to occur over a cup of tea at the kitchen table

with other women present. This style of working is adopted for a
number of reasons. First, as I have previously indicated, the organization feels that formal counselling would shift the balance of power
away from the woman. Second, individual sessions between women
and workers would detract from the group dynamic of the safe
house. Working with the group of residents is a way of modelling
the belief that domestic violence is a social and political concern; it
does not happen to women in isolation. The organization feels that
individual sessions would model the belief that it occurs as a result
of an individual woman's pathology, and they would not wish to
convey this.

Enabling women to make informed choices about their future requires skilled listening and also the provision of information about
the range of options open to the woman. The complexity of the
effects of violence requires a high degree of sensitivity. Within the
refuge setting a woman is likely to experience for the first time responsibility for acting for herself rather than acting as her male partner wishes. She will be making many major decisions in choosing
to leave her partner permanently and this is never straightforward.
The woman will have been threatened with being found if she ever
attempts to leave and might live in fear of being traced and pun-
ished. For some the unknown is more frightening than what is
known, although the known is uncomfortable and potentially life
threatening. A small percentage of women feel they must return
to their partners. Whatever decision a woman makes it is the aim
of the Woman's Aid worker to provide an opportunity to explore
her options, helped by an accepting, non-judgemental attitude. The
central concern is that the woman makes the decision that is right
for her. Women who decide to leave their partners and therefore
move on to the second stage accommodation and await rehousing,
are likely to need much support. Having made such a major step
only to be faced with a lengthy wait to be rehoused, is depressing
and disheartening. Living with other women in the house might be
acceptable and reassuring for the woman in a crisis, but becomes
less attractive as a long-term prospect. Workers find their awareness of this process of the woman's mixed and changing feelings
helps them support her at this point.

RAPE CRISIS CENTRES

Rape Crisis Centres were first set up during the mid-1970s, following increased awareness of another form of violence perpetrated on

women. More became known about what is 'the greatest possible invasion of a woman's body and self against her wishes and without her consent' (Walker 1990: 163). The Women's Movement increased consciousness about the nature and prevalence of rape, and of women's silence about it. The amount of reported rape was recognized as the tip of the iceberg with the vast majority of offences going unreported. Myths about rape and stereotypes about women who are raped, began to be explored and exploded. The dismissive attitudes towards this crime shown by both the police and the judiciary highlighted further how victims of violence were being victimized yet again by being blamed for it.

Rape Crisis Centres were set up as women-only groups to provide a counselling service to women victims of rape. They were established as collectives, although some centres have since initiated management committee structures as it was felt that long-term planning and policy making could more easily be achieved within this structure. The creation of management committees freed both paid workers and volunteer counsellors so that their meeting time together could examine the quality and operation of the current service rather than work on business decisions. Local Rape Crisis Centres are autonomous, and not all operate in the same way. There are differences in funding, size of project, and how the counselling service is operated. There are also differences of degree in philosophical outlook with a range of Feminist perspectives being expressed and adopted. How this affects counselling will be explored in Chapter 6.

Some projects are located within a town's Women's Centre. Some centres operate a home-counselling service where, for reasons of safety, two counsellors visit clients together. Others insist that counselling takes place at the centre believing that a woman needs a neutral place in which to discuss and express her feelings about the experience of such abusive violence. Additionally her commitment to coming for counselling rather than counselling coming to her is seen as significant in the woman's journey of beginning to look after herself and value herself again. Rape and domestic violence both make women feel dirty, worthless, and that they are not worth caring for or about, and carefully challenging this is one aim of a Rape Crisis Centre.

Funding of the centres comes from city and county councils. During the early 1990s, and in common with other voluntary agencies and charities, increasingly and of necessity centres have had to obtain funds from other sources. For example Friends' groups are encouraged and these are primarily for fund raising. Income from schemes such as 'Opportunities for Volunteers', funded through the Department of Health, is well used and much needed. These schemes provide a time-limited grant, usually three years, in the expectation that further funding will be sought from elsewhere at the end of that period. Projects having access to such funding are able to employ paid workers who, in turn, train and supervise more volunteers. To illustrate the philosophies and policies of these centres, I will describe in detail how one organizes its counselling service.

Derby Rape Crisis Centre

This Rape Crisis Centre has been operating for a number of years. It has an extensive, well-established counselling service in an area which has little other counselling provision (Derby Rape Crisis Annual Report 1991). There are three paid workers, and a number of volunteer counsellors who are called unpaid workers. Unpaid workers counsel women and operate telephone help-lines at speci-fied times, and have a commitment to weekly meetings and month-ly supervision. Other workers look after children while mothers receive counselling.

The Centre is housed in the town's Women's Centre, a large house near the centre of town which serves as an umbrella organ-ization for a number of women-only groups. The house is warm and welcoming. There are a number of comfortably furnished small rooms, as well as a few larger rooms suitable for meetings or groups. Small rooms are furnished with large floor cushions only; it is felt that the non-hierarchical nature of the working relationship is modelled in the seating arrangements. However such furnishing can pose difficulties for older women who are arthritic or those with disabilities.

Counselling service

The unpaid workers come from a range of different backgrounds and cultures. There has been an emphasis on recruiting Asian and Afro-Caribbean workers so that the counsellors reflect more ac-curately the cultural mix of the population that is being served. Counsellors commit themselves to a sixteen-week training pro-gramme and on-going supervision. Most workers receive counsel-ling themselves and this is seen as beneficial overall. The Centre has an arrangement with local counsellors who offer a reduced rate or a free service to Rape Crisis counsellors. The physical setting of the centre, with its small, private, quiet and attractive rooms as well as a women-only environment is seen as ideal for the facilitation of the counselling process. In exceptional circumstances, women can be offered a home-based service. This would be so in the case of women who are agoraphobic (a symptom of sexual abuse), and disabled women.

Counselling models

The belief that rape of women can only be understood within a social and political context is fundamental to the counselling work of any Rape Crisis Centre. Rape is seen as an extreme example of the way in which men exert power over women in our society. Women clients are 'encouraged to explore the nature of the social relations between men and women which generates male violence' (Dryden *et al*. 1989: 25). The counselling of rape victims is firmly set within a social context of the oppression of women within society. Without this, it is thought that the counsellor can collude with the belief that the individual's distress is her problem alone: again blaming the victim for the problem and minimizing the role of the offender.

In common with other Rape Crisis Centres and organizations, from the late 1980s onwards, this Centre has been affected by the numbers of women seeking counselling as survivors of childhood sexual abuse. At one time, being a survivor would be disclosed during the counselling process. Women are now more likely to request counselling directly because of childhood abuse. No other agency in the locality offers such a counselling service so the Rape Crisis Centre has become the agency offering this specialist provision.

The counselling models that are found useful are person-centred, Gestalt, and, to a more limited extent, Transactional Analysis. All the work of the Centre, and therefore all counselling is informed by a Feminist perspective, which cuts across theoretical perspectives. The choice of counselling models is primarily due to worker preference, but also reflects both the counselling training available locally and those used by their external supervisors, as well as better meeting the needs of this client group. The person-centred approach encourages the woman to be in charge of her own counselling process, believing that she is the expert in her own healing. This is a central theme in all Feminist perspectives, whatever the theoretical stance. For example, Women's Therapy Centres are primarily psychodynamic in approach, but hold fiercely to the tenet that the client is expert in her own healing. This dynamic is important in any counselling where the content is of violence or sexual abuse towards the client either as an adult or child. The use of Gestalt exercises can help women get in touch with hidden feelings or memories they may have dissociated from and the 'two-chair exercise', described more fully in Chapter 3, can assist clients in confronting their abusers in the safety of the counselling room rather than in real situations. Such action-based exercises work well when the counselling is about reactions to trauma: they can engage the client and enable her to get in touch with repressed feelings and then allow their expression.

HOME-START

Home-Start is an organization through which volunteers, usually parents themselves, befriend families of pre-school age children. It was formed by an individual, Margaret Harrison, in Leicester in 1973. Margaret Harrison had professional and personal experiences with mothers, and saw a need for providing extra support for socially isolated families and those in difficulty and crisis. In 1978 there was a single scheme in Leicester: by 1991 there were 141 schemes in the UK and abroad including schemes in Australia and Quebec and in Israel, in both Jewish and Arab communities (Home-Start 1990). Home-Start is another organization set up by a woman of vision who by using and valuing her personal and professional experience recognized a gap in statutory provision in services for women and acted accordingly.

Although Home-Start was set up to work with families and parents, it works primarily with mothers, and practically all the volunteers and organizers are women. In its home visiting scheme, Home-Start aims to offer support, friendship and practical assistance to young families. Counselling is not an aim of the scheme, but listening is emphasized. Volunteers are envisaged as being 'alongside' families in this particular phase of their development. This aspect is crucial and is explored in more detail later in the chapter. A Home-Start organizer explained her thinking:

'The focus of the scheme is working through parents to the children: the reason for supporting families is so that children do not miss out developmentally. Having said that, we recognize that unless a parent herself is cared for, she cannot care for her children. Parenting is about self-esteem, confidence and the adult's needs being met, otherwise a child cannot be adequately cared for.'

Each local Home-Start is representative of its community, in that it has local funding, volunteers and management committee members. Each Home-Start has at least one paid organizer, a group of volunteers, and is managed by a multi-disciplinary committee. Funding is usually through an annually renewable Agreement with the Local Authority, from either Health, Social Services, or Education. Extra funding might come from local businesses and trusts.

Emphasis is placed on the training and support of volunteers; in this way volunteers are 'looked after' so they can 'look after' mothers who look after children. Families are referred by health visitors, social workers, or through self-referral. It is felt that the success of Home-Start arises from careful matching of a particular volunteer to a particular family – just as families come from all walks of life, so do volunteers, and careful pairing is considered imperative. Volunteers befriend a small number of families whom they visit at home, usually weekly. Being a professional friend means that extra support and visiting can be offered through the scheme when it is needed. As such, a Home-Start volunteer liaises with staff such as health visitors and social workers and makes referrals on behalf of the adults in the families.

Use of counselling skills within Home-Start

Home-Start, like Women's Aid, is very clear that counselling is not an aim. For both organizations, counselling is seen as too formal an activity: it would set up a certain sort of relationship between the two women which would not reflect the organization's aims. However, both organizations are equally clear that the use of counselling skills is fundamental to them. The volunteer's course of preparation includes training in counselling skills. In all of the training, both the preparation course and the on-going training days, good listening is a ground rule for the teaching group. Home-Start models 'good parenting' in the way that befrienders nurture mothers and families that are visited. As a reflection of this, good listening is modelled during training courses and organizers' relationships with volunteers. Home-Start organizers are experienced in using counselling skills. In this way Home-Start is similar to other women's organizations: there is a feeling of 'wholeness' about it; a feeling of congruence. 'Good parenting' and 'good listening' permeate the whole organization.

In a book that evaluates Home-Start during its first four years, William Van der Eyken (1982: 65) considers the nature of 'mothering' and explores whether or not Home-Start volunteers should be considered as therapists. He argues that in a number of aspects they operate in the same way as therapists, in terms of function and aims for the work. Van der Eyken argues that the 'being with' function of psychotherapy is the same as the 'being alongside' function of the befrienders. 'Being with' demands a high degree of empathy with the client. It demands constancy and consistency, and genuineness on the part of the therapist and he sees these as the essential qualities of a befriender. Van der Eyken goes on to quote the work of Sydney Bloch (1977: 63–7) who describes the contract established between the therapist and client as one 'whose objectives are the alleviation of distress, the improved functioning of the family and the better adaptive coping with stress'. Again the parallel is made with the aims of the Home-Start volunteer in her work with families. Rather than compare these volunteers with therapists, I would describe their work as principally and centrally incorporating good listening skills. Further, a high proportion of a Home-Start volunteer's work with women is re-parenting. For women whose experience of childhood was of faulty or abusive parenting, the opportunity of being in such a restorative relationship is crucial. It offers and creates a healing process and leads to development and personal growth. Being befriended by a volunteer enables a socially isolated woman to lead a more fulfilling and healthy life, and helps her to be part of a more extensive social network. Brown and Harris's work (1978) on depression among mothers clearly demonstrated that the lack of meaningful relationships, with both partners and friends, was one of the predisposing factors leading to depression in women. By the sensitive use of counselling skills, a Home-Start volunteer engages the woman she is working with in a relationship which is therapeutic for the client. Through this she can reach the point when she is able to make greater use of professional and formal services, including counselling. Women who would have been unlikely to have gone to a counselling agency, and have been unable to engage in the counselling process, can be helped to do so where this is appropriate because of their involvement in Home-Start.

Women users of both Home-Start and Women's Aid have been given the opportunity to be engaged in helping relationships. These have prepared the ground for possible future counselling by emphasizing and offering empathic listening. They can thus exercise the option of becoming involved in counselling if they choose to. It seems that for many women, subject to particular life experiences, there needs to be a supportive first stage which prepares them for later engagement in the more formal process of counselling and which helps them to maximize its potential.

FAMILY CENTRES

Family Centres are a resource for families with children under five. Some are attached to nurseries funded by Social Services Departments, whilst others are purpose-built so that nursery provision is integrated within the Family Centre. Part of their function is the provision of community resources, which are open to all, not just to parents of young children. The Centre will house a whole range of community groups as well as legal advice sessions, women's health projects and adult education classes. There are likely to be women-only groups, women-only classes, and specialist women-only projects. Some Centres incorporated the provision of a counselling service and many offer specialist counselling for women survivors of childhood abuse, and for women who are depressed or who have been referred by the psychiatric services.

Family Centres were set up in response to reports such as the Plowden Report (Plowden 1967) which emphasized the importance of pre-school age provision, both educational and social, for children. The aims of the early Family Centres were very similar to those of Home-Start which was conceived at the same time and in tune with the same social thinking. The emphasis was on providing resources for parents (usually mothers) so that the children could be helped through their mothers. Family Centres set up in the 1980s seem to have shifted focus: a greater emphasis is placed on the woman user of the service herself, that is as a carer. Thus a Family Centre of the 1980s might make a much stronger statement about a woman's right to work, therefore accepting the principle that nursery provision will sometimes be for the children of working mothers. When a Family Centre has this philosophy there will be even greater emphasis on adult education provision.

Pen Green Family Centre

One example of a Family Centre with an effective counselling service is that of the pioneering Pen Green Family Centre, set up in 1983 (Wallis 1992). It has four strands to its work, reflecting its funding. It was originally funded by the Departments of Education, Social Services, and Health. It therefore consisted of a community nursery, a social work service to mothers and families, a health centre and a community education programme. Its staff team is a multi-disciplinary one. It was established after the local community in Corby was identified as an area of social deprivation. Corby is a predominately Glaswegian community in the East Midlands which has a long history of active community participation and action.

Counselling provision at Pen Green

The local area had few voluntary organizations in the early 1980s. There were no national voluntary organizations providing counselling in the immediate area (for example, Family Welfare Association, Family Service Unit, or Marriage Guidance Council (Relate)). Because of the lack of local counselling provision, counselling and the provision of a counselling service was a major aim of the Centre. Owing to the lack of mental health services for women locally, counselling tended to concentrate on women who were depressed or who were referred from the psychiatric services. In the later 1980s, with the explosion of disclosure by adults, primarily women, of sexual abuse in childhood a specialist counselling service for survivors then developed.

As counselling was a central aim from the outset, considerable thought was given to the training of staff and volunteers. Family Centres frequently use volunteers, 'Family Friends', similar to Home-Start volunteers, but who have more involvement in other Centre activities. It was felt important that all employed staff should have their own particular training profile. A system was developed whereby all staff and volunteers would have some counselling skills training, and other staff (including the secretaries and receptionists who were seen as essential front-line workers), would be expected to have further training. Staff training was given a high profile as was the opportunity for staff to be involved in self-awareness and team-building days. An important, although sadly unusual principle, was that staff would be funded to have their own counselling and allowed time during the working day for this. This counselling was not available for all staff but was available for those in need due to particular stresses at work or at home. Such counselling for staff was viewed as part of a staff-care package. (Generally Public Service organizations are slow at offering such a service for staff in the UK, one significant exception being the Education Service of the Royal Borough of Kensington and Chelsea (Casemore 1991, personal communication)).

In a busy Family Centre, well used by members of the community, it is difficult setting up formal counselling sessions. Often, opening contacts are made to staff members while talking in corridors or in discussions about children. Staff need to be sensitive to the requests for counselling and to set up clear boundaries. Clients are quickly

invited to somewhere more private and the possibility of formal
sessions explained. Rooms are set aside for counselling and everyone in the Centre respects the 'Do not disturb' notices. Boundary
setting was carefully instituted from the early days of the organization. Without this counselling could easily have been overwhelmed
by the other activities in the Centre. As part of a response to the
ever-increasing requests for counselling by women survivors, an
on-going therapy group was also set up.

The counselling models used once again reflect availability and
worker preference. Much of the counselling training was from
National Marriage Guidance (Relate) using Egan's model (1986)
and was psychodynamically orientated. Some workers were also
trained and interested in the use of Gestalt techniques. Some members of the staff team, although not all, were and are Feminists in
that they had 'a heightened awareness of the psychological effects
of social conditioning, sex-roles, and women's second class status'
(Carob 1987: 29).

Much of the work of the counselling service is in the areas of
childhood abuse and depression but women are also encouraged
and supported in exploring all aspects of their selves. The issues that
arise in individual counselling are often translated into a groupwork or educational context. For example, the need for a forum in
which women could explore female sexuality was recognized and a
course was set up for this purpose. In this way movement is encouraged and facilitated between counselling and educational provision.
General issues that arise in counselling can be translated into an
educational context, and conversely educational learning that trig-
gers personal issues can be addressed by the provision of counselling.

FAMILY SERVICE UNITS

Family Service Units is a national organization. It is a voluntary
social work agency registered as a charity. It grew out of the Pacifist
Service Units during World War II which provided a practical social
work service to bombed out families. There are presently twenty
one Units in England and one in Scotland offering a social work service to distressed and troubled families who live in areas of urban
deprivation. A number of Units have set up specialist Women's Counselling Projects. Some are culture-specific, for example, the Asian
and Chinese Women's Counselling Projects; others are community-
based projects and some specialize in offering a counselling service
to women survivors of childhood abuse. Those projects which are

not culture-specific are multi-cultural services and are engaged in trans-cultural counselling.

Family Service Units, although a national organization, are individually managed by management committees made up from representatives of the local community and statutory organizations. Each Unit is usually housed in a large ordinary house, incorporated into the community in which it is based. Units are funded, in the main, through Agreements with local authorities, but like other charities and voluntary organizations in the late 1980s and early 1990s, there has been a short-fall in local authority funding and fund raising has been undertaken in earnest. During the period 1988–92 three Units have closed through lack of funding.

Women's Counselling Projects in Family Service Units

The Women's Counselling Projects grew mainly from three different sorts of needs. First, Family Service Units, like other organizations working with women, were bombarded by disclosures of childhood abuse by women from the mid 1980s onward, and with these disclosures, requests for counselling. Some Units specialized in working with families where physical and/or sexual abuse of children had occurred. Usually these Units were specially funded to work in this area. Those Units soon found that practically all of the mothers of abused children had been sexually abused themselves as children: these women increasingly asked for counselling for themselves. Family Service Units are characteristically part of their local community and, as part of their role, establish community services not already available. Thus community-based counselling services for women arose from a perceived lack of community-based mental health provision. For women to make maximum use of mental health services, they need to be situated within travelling distance from them. Women's role as family carers and the complications inherent in that role mean that geography can be vital in determining whether or not services are genuinely accessible. The studies indicating a higher incidence of depression in working class women with young children were also considered. Last, culture-specific counselling projects were set up in ways that enabled women of the particular culture to feel comfortable in using them. Barriers relating to language difficulties or understanding cultural nuances could be dismantled. Most counselling projects are set up and organized by Family Service Unit staff who are themselves counsellors and the services develop through training and supervision programmes for women volunteer counsellors who work in them.

Counselling considerations

Many of the counselling considerations within Women's Counselling Projects at Family Service Units will be the same as in other women's organizations. But I will explore ways in which the Family Service Units context is somewhat different. The central difference is that these projects set out to work in a multi-cultural context, although within that some of the projects are culture-specific. In this way Asian and Chinese women counsellors work with Asian and Chinese clients to avoid the language difficulties and cultural nuances referred to above.

A clinical example

An Asian counsellor working with an Asian woman who has been labelled as having a psychiatric illness will be aware of cultural factors that might come into play. Depression can result from a confusion of cultural identities, and, for example, post-natal depression in a young Asian mother with a newborn baby may stem from her attempts to act in ways which are acceptable in her culture. However white professionals may expect and pressurize her to behave in ways acceptable to them. She is instantly caught in a culture clash at a time when she is at her most vulnerable. Within an Asian extended family the feeding programme of babies might be the concern of the whole family, whereas outside professional workers might feel this should be the mother's sole responsibility. And so this unfortunate new mother is caught in the middle of the expectations of two different cultures and depression may result. If workers are not culture-sensitive they may define her depression incorrectly, and respond inappropriately.

A second example relates to counselling an Asian woman sexually abused as a child. Inevitably the counselling process takes longer than with a white woman. There will be enormous difficulty in arriving at disclosure. Child sexual abuse is a taboo subject and there is no language to enable her to be sexually explicit – it simply does not exist. This is further exacerbated in that in this instance the client is part of an extended family network, and cannot simply be viewed as an autonomous individual. In any individual's situation considerations about other family members have to be taken into account, but this is sharply highlighted in a culture where a powerful extended family is the norm. In addition, in a woman's healing process, the experience of racism has to be taken on board as yet another abuse, an abuse woven deeply into the structure of society.

In projects that are set up for women from different cultures, a counsellor will work with women from the same culture as herself as well as with women from others. When working cross-culturally, the fact that the counsellor belongs to a different culture needs always to be acknowledged. A client should not however be expected to teach a counsellor about her culture: counsellors should take responsibility for educating themselves about the whole range of different cultures they may encounter. Counsellors should also be aware of the class differences in British society and how each class has a culture of its own. In this context, the emphasis is on how women experience being a member of a particular class.

Racism is an issue that must be on the counselling agenda between counsellor and client. To what extent it is part of the counselling dynamic should be explored within the counselling relationship. White counsellors need to be aware that it is painful and difficult to hear about the experiences of racist abuse their black clients have been subjected to. Counsellors who work in multi-cultural settings in contrast to those working in culture-specific ones, tend to hold the belief that between women there is a universal language, and that although cultural differences are important they can be over-come because our experiences as women unite us.

WOMEN'S THERAPY CENTRES

In any examination of counselling in women's organizations, Women's Therapy Centres are in a field of their own. They are unique in being established and organized to provide a therapy service for women, rather than using counselling skills in response to particular problems or situations.

Many of the Centres started life, as did the London Centre, in a room in a therapist's house, while funding was obtained for larger premises. Now they inhabit a floor, sometimes two, in build-ings which house a range of other organizations. Some Centres, for example, the Leeds Women's Therapy Centre juggle limited room space by very careful organization and the employment of thera-pists on a sessional rather than full-time basis. Funding for Centres comes from Local Authority sources, Trusts, and fees on a sliding scale from those clients who can afford to pay. Funding has been a major difficulty in the early 1990s, in common with other organ-izations discussed earlier in this chapter. Special fund raising drives

have been undertaken, and some Centres now only employ sessional staff as a way of saving money as well as space. The therapeutic services on offer in Centres are: individual therapy; group
therapy; theme-centred groups and workshops; and sometimes,
couples counselling. In addition Centres have evolved their own
training packages for professional workers working with women.

Therapy or counselling?

Some Centres, such as Birmingham Women's Therapy Centre, clearly
specify that they offer a long-term psychotherapy service for women,
not counselling. In the main, in all Centres, the therapeutic work
that goes on, in the form of individual and group therapy, is long-
term, that is, it lasts for at least a year, and usually two or three.
This longer term work models the belief that a woman should be
valued for who she is as a person, and not just treated as a role or
a problem. Thus Women's Therapy Centres believe that theme-
focused counselling addresses one aspect of women's lives but that
a woman is more than her status as a survivor or as someone with
an eating disorder. It is felt that long-term therapy counteracts the
socializing experiences of women which results in them feeling
'unworthy, undeserving and unentitled' (Eichenbaum and Orbach
1983: 13). Women come to believe that they are not important in
themselves for themselves.

The differences between counselling and psychotherapy continues to be a significant debating point, and there exists no single,
simple answer (Dryden *et al.* 1989: 7 and Hooper and Dryden 1991:
5). Therapists within Women's Therapy Centres seem clearer about
these differences, perhaps because they are trained in the psychodynamic school. It can be argued that the therapist concentrates
on a client's inner world, whereas the counsellor focuses on helping
the client resolve both external and internal issues which are gen-
erating problems for that client. Also, it is arguable that Feminist
therapists are not concerned solely with inner worlds but are
constantly aware of the complicated interface between the inner
world and outer political and social realities, as well as the reality
of relationships. For the psychodynamically trained therapist the
focus of the work lies in the transference between therapist and
client, whereas for the counsellor this is not necessarily the case.
These ideas are explored further in Chapter 3.

The question arises of how to respond to the woman who may
not want long-term help. One response is to offer short-term counselling in the form of a crisis service, such as in operation at the

Leeds Centre. This can be offered almost immediately and the therapist contracts with the client to see her for a limited number of sessions, six to eight, over whatever time scale seems appropriate to the client. By confining the counselling service to such a limited contract, therapists are able to keep the distinction between counselling and therapy very clear. The short-term counselling will have another function in that it will be used as a method of assessing whether or not a woman would wish to, or be able to, work in a longer term way. However there is clearly a grey area on the counselling and therapy continuum. It may be that some workers designated as counsellors actually move into psychotherapy with some of their clients, and the reverse can also be true. Many believe there is no absolute dividing line between the two modes. As ever, what is important is that appropriate help is offered to women. How that help is labelled is a very secondary consideration.

The enormous demand for individual therapy could lead to two-year waiting lists (Krzowski and Land 1988: 3), which was clearly unsatisfactory, and the London Workshop Programme was devised to meet this demand:

> Certain themes came up in individual sessions again and again, themes that seemed part of the very fabric of being a woman in this society: pain and anger between mothers and daughters, tensions about dependency and independence, huge problems over separation, anxieties over sexuality, feelings about being in a caring role and not being allowed to have needs. It was decided to set up short, time-limited groups that would focus specifically on certain of these issues as a way of raising awareness, giving specific help and enabling women to decide what further steps they might take to help themselves.
>
> (Krzowski and Land 1988: 4)

Therapeutic models

The orientation of women therapists employed by Women's Therapy Centres is primarily psychodynamic. Although Centres will inevitably be influenced by the focus of the local psychotherapy courses which are training future therapists, the favoured school within the psychodynamic tradition is that of Object Relations (Eichenbaum and Orbach 1983: 13). This is a model of psychological development in which the first two years of a person's life are seen as the most important time in the development of personality and psyche. This early development is further seen to be in the context of relationships and the impact of those on the person. Newborn babies enter a social world and have the capacity to become part of human culture. The social context into which a girl child is born, the child-rearing patterns and gender arrangements which are a function of that society thus have an impact on her personality development and upon her 'inner world'.

Training in Object Relations psychotherapy is a foundation for many Feminist therapists. However Women's Therapy Centres themselves have been instrumental in developing thinking about women's psychological development, and the issues women bring to counselling. They have been influenced by the impact of women writers such as Phyllis Chesler (1972: 4), whose 'illuminating study of women and the mental health establishment', pioneered studies which explored women's experiences of psychologists, psychiatrists, and psychoanalysts, and how sexist attitudes in the clinical treatment of women were maintained. Writers such as Nancy Chodorow (1978: 77) began to explore the meaning and impact of the mother–daughter relationship, and how critical this relationship is in the developing girl's sense of self. Writers from Women's Therapy Centres are part of a movement that has applied Feminist thinking to psychoanalytic ideas, alongside writers such as Juliet Mitchell (1975), Nancy Chodorow (1978) and Dorothy Dinnerstein (1978), all influenced by aspects of Freudian theory. This innovative thinking should not be underestimated in its radical re-thinking about women's psychology. It has been undertaken by therapists, sometimes as individuals, but more often in conjunction with groups of women colleagues, and has represented a major challenge to traditional views that cannot be ignored. The knowledge has been disseminated both by writing and by setting up their own Women's Therapy training programmes. There are courses in Feminist psychodynamic psychotherapy as well as courses which examine issues for women counsellors and therapists working with women clients. However the work done by this group of Feminist psychotherapists has had significant and wide-ranging implications for psychotherapy as a whole.

Counselling within women's organizations inevitably has many similarities. The same counselling models are appropriate even when the problems are different. All of the projects base their work with women on an understanding of women's experience within society today, whether this is overtly stated or not. Some projects name this understanding of women as Feminist, others do not. The whole range of Feminist views exists within the projects: the implications of this for counselling are explored in Chapter 6. All the organizations work in similar ways; often the difference is one of emphasis. For example, whereas all organizations wish their services to be accessible to women from different cultures and social classes and take steps to ensure that their environment is inviting to all women, Family Service Units are proactive in ensuring that their counselling service is multi-cultural. The difference between organizations in this instance is one of degree.

The significance of the Women's Therapy Centres is far-reaching. Indeed all the developments outlined in this chapter are positive and exciting. They represent an enormous challenge to traditional ways of working with and understanding women. All the projects are examples of women working with women, in ways which appreciate, value and validate the characteristics and strengths of women. Women are being taken seriously and at last the possibility exists that women's needs and circumstances can be properly and effectively acknowledged and addressed in counselling and therapy. Perhaps most importantly women are being enabled to take themselves seriously; to value themselves and their contributions in their own right. They are beginning to see themselves not as supporting members of the cast but as centre-stage.

THREE

The practice of counselling women

In this chapter I examine issues common to counselling, and how these are highlighted by the context, that of working with women. Boundary issues are considered from a number of aspects, and I then explore the use of different counselling models in women's organizations. Selection and supervision of counsellors is described, and finally issues of gender, class and culture are considered.

BOUNDARIES

A key area in any discussion about counselling issues is that of boundaries. Where, when, and for how long, does counselling take place? In organizations where counselling is just one of many activities, how is counselling marked out and distinguished from those other activities? How are boundaries relating to possible role conflicts approached? These may be relatively straightforward, but others such as those between counselling and psychotherapy (discussed in Chapter 2) or between counselling and the use of counselling skills, are more complicated.

In the context of counselling women, the issue of boundaries is not only an obvious place to start but is essential. For women the question of blurred boundaries is a central theme in their lives:

> women's psychology is one of unclear boundaries, of an insecure or illusive sense of self. Women often search for themselves in their relationships with others, seeking definition in contact. The central aspect of women's psychology, the one that embodies most of the major themes, is the lack

of psychological separateness, the absence of boundaries within which a secure sense of self is contained.

(Eichenbaum and Orbach 1983: 138)

Women are brought up to be accommodating, to put other people's needs before their own. They are expected to merge with other people, to be responsible for other people's needs. They are not expected to set clear, firm boundaries for themselves and around themselves. There is a social pressure on women to be caring and giving. A woman who states her own clear personal boundaries, about what she is prepared to do and not do, is seen as non-caring (Chaplin 1988b: 100–10).

A major reason why this issue looms so large in women's lives is because of their reproductive function. The unique experience for women is their ability to be pregnant and give birth. At birth the physical differentiation of mother and child begins. The emotional separateness of the two is a complex and on-going process. Further, women who have been subject to violence or childhood abuse, have had their own personal boundaries trampled on and interfered with in an horrific and extreme manner. It will therefore be inevitable that, in counselling women, boundary issues need to be addressed in some form or another and often in many. It will also be necessary to maintain firm boundaries within the counselling. I will now explore in more detail some key features relating to this central issue.

Setting

Where counselling takes place is the first boundary that the client encounters. The setting itself models the counselling provision it offers. This section explores the importance of environment in the provision of counselling for women. Workers in Women's Therapy Centres, Rape Crisis, Women's Aid, and Family Centres consciously make the place as welcoming and pro-women as possible. Posters and notices and the way women are welcomed and addressed carry implicit messages. Putting them at their ease, perhaps offering them a cup of tea when they arrive, are ways of nurturing clients (Chaplin 1988b: 25), and are particularly important for women who spend much of their time nurturing and looking after other people.

This emphasis on welcoming women in their initial encounter with the organization has not been evident in white, male, Eurocentric models of counselling, with its emphasis on 'getting down to business' straight away. When counselling women from unfamiliar cultures it will be necessary to be aware of the culture-specific social conventions in greeting and meeting with women. Some time may be spent observing these conventions before embarking on more formal counselling. For instance, as noted in Chapter 2, if the content of the counselling is a taboo subject within the culture, such as childhood abuse, then care and time have to be taken before these issues can be explored.

The theories on which many counselling models are based project both masculine and western cultural images. Developmental theorists, such as Freud and Erikson, build upon the development of male children. Experiences of male childhood and adulthood are taken as the norm. Female development is different. Whereas, for example, separation and individuation are of critical importance for boys and men, since separation from mother is essential to the development of masculinity, for women this is not the case. The creation of feminine identity does not depend on separation: women value connectedness and relatedness.

> But in this light, the conception of development itself also depends on the context in which it is framed, and the vision of maturity can be seen to shift when adulthood is portrayed by women rather than men. When women construct the adult domain, the world of relationships emerges and becomes the focus of attention and concern.
>
> (Gilligan 1982: 167)

When women counsel women, they 'get down to business' in a different way from men. A little time is taken to establish the foundations of the relationship: to find connections. Gillian talked of this difference when she visited her woman counsellor:

> 'I just couldn't get started when I went to see Martin. The first time I went to see him I was very anxious, thinking about what I wanted to talk about. I made some comment about the riding gear he had in the hall. I love riding and I was desperately trying to make connections with him: it would have made me feel more comfortable. Later in that session he made a comment about me trying to get too friendly with him by finding out about his family's hobbies.'
>
> (Personal communication)

The male counsellor's response implied that Gillian's opening remarks were undermining the professional relationship, whereas a woman counsellor would interpret them as a way of connecting in order to build the professional relationship.

Some organizations offer a wholly women-only environment. Organizations which do not may set aside room space so that a women-only environment can be provided, on one floor or in one wing of the building. Often, rooms designated for counselling will be decorated and wallpapered to resemble homes rather than in-stitutions. The message is that here woman meets woman, and not that patient meets expert. Rooms which are multi-purpose indicate when they are in use for counselling. However this is done, staff learn during their induction period never to interrupt if the 'Engaged' sign is on the door. Similarly a counselling session is protected from interruption by telephone calls. In settings solely designed for coun-selling or therapy, these features become second-nature, and are central to its ethos. When counselling is one activity amongst others, a conscious effort is required to ensure that all staff respect these basic boundaries.

Confidentiality

The boundary of confidentiality exists for all women seeking help. For some, particularly those subject to violence and childhood abuse, or those who experience themselves as objects rather than people, this will be new. It will be the first time she is valued enough to be granted confidentiality. It will be the first time another has not insisted that he, or unusually she, has the right to her thoughts and her experiences.

Organizations have to clearly consider their policy on confiden-tiality. Where counselling is one service among others that are offered, care has to be taken that content from counselling sessions is kept separate from other community activity and knowledge. Sometimes, confidentiality is a particular issue at the beginning of counselling when client and counsellor are from the same culture. Asian women working with Asian counsellors, for example, may need considerable reassurance that confidentiality is absolutely re-spected, particularly if they are from the same community. There can be an assumption or even an expectation that confidentiality is not total and may be broken. One Asian counsellor talking about assessment procedures explained that she spent time with some clients checking out who was related to whom and what social relationships they had in common. If the client felt uncomfortable with the degree of social closeness she would be referred to another counsellor.

Groups which cannot guarantee confidentiality advise workers to explain this early in the contact. Within Women's Aid and

Home-Start, workers explain to women what records will be kept, what information might be disclosed to others and why this would be done. In Women's Aid women are seen by different workers on different occasions – a form of serial counselling – and detailed records are kept so that information is easily passed on. This is explained to women at the outset and they are asked for their permission for records to be kept. In some projects for abuse survivors, or Family Centres, records are only kept of basic information (for example, address, number of children, GP), but there will be no records relating either to the counselling or to past history. It is thought preferable to keep records to a minimum because of the specific content of the counselling.

Women's Aid and Rape Crisis workers are provided with a high degree of support and supervision. Feelings about the work can be discussed and off-loaded within this supportive network. This is seen as important for a number of reasons. One is an attempt to ensure that distressing but confidential information is kept within the organization rather than taken outside. This would clearly be a danger if sufficient support was not available. Immediately after counselling sessions, Rape Crisis workers de-brief with their support worker or supervisor, giving an opportunity to talk about the sessions and feelings aroused in a general way which does not necessarily reveal the client's identity.

Early in their training, volunteers are taught about the necessity for confidentiality and the potential difficulties of working in a small, close-knit, local community. They will explore confidentiality in all its aspects. Although volunteers usually recognize that information about clients is never divulged in social situations, they may not have considered the further complexities of the situation. These include questions relating to divulging information to statutory agencies, for example the police or social services, and how to respond to a client's relatives and friends who may make contact asking advice about helping the client (Scottish Women's Aid 1991: 53). These dilemmas are explored in training by incorporating role-plays, so that volunteers are clear when they face these in reality.

The question of when to break confidentiality is faced by all organizations. This is highlighted when information is given to a counsellor revealing danger either to a client or to another person. Some organizations are required to follow child protection guidelines; others are not bound by these. They have to decide if they will encourage clients to disclose child abuse to the statutory agencies, or whether they take an active role themselves to 'report' it. The implications of this decision are immense. In counselling, a woman

is treated with respect and as someone of intrinsic value. If she is
then suddenly placed in a situation where the needs of a child are
paramount, she may feel yet again that her value and importance
is only secondary. At the same time organizations genuinely wish
to protect children from abuse. The dilemma is great and there are
no simple answers. The following illustrates these difficulties: Mary
disclosed during counselling that her 15-year old sister was still
being sexually abused by their uncle. Mary was 18 and the counsellor
was aware how difficult it had been for her to refer herself. There
had been a number of false starts; she came late or cancelled appointments. She was the eldest daughter who had been expected to
be responsible for her younger siblings, and deny her own needs.
The agency policy on child protection was that such situations must
be referred to Social Services. Yet the counsellor was aware what
this would mean for Mary: her entitlement to time for herself would
once more be overshadowed by the needs of her sister. Inevitably
counselling time would be taken up with exploring and gaining
information about the abuse. There was a very real possibility that
Mary would drop out of counselling, when matters were taken out
of her hands and control, and at home she would have to attend
to all the ramifications disclosure would mean.

Working with partners

From time to time the possibility of working with a woman's
partner arises, perhaps following a direct request from the woman
herself. Organizations differ as to how this possibility is viewed.
Some, such as Rape Crisis, are clear that they are women-only
organizations, providing a service only to women. Other organizations acknowledge that, at times, working with the woman and her
partner is a way of helping her, by tackling the interaction which
may be causing her distress or contributing to the present difficulty.
A Survivors Counselling Project might as policy offer the possibility
of couples counselling, believing this to be of assistance to the women
users. Another alternative is that the partner may be seen by another worker, perhaps with a view to working for a specified number
of sessions in a foursome.

Problem or person?

All the organizations discussed in this book acknowledge that the
service that they offer is not one that stays focused solely on the presenting problem. Women's Aid workers find that in looking after

women in refuges they are not dealing just with the aftermath of violence. They discover that the experience of trauma stirs up much concerning a woman's past history and how she has been treated all her life. This is particularly so if this is the first time that a woman has been related to as a person in her own right. Home-Start volunteers find that they cannot fulfil one of the main aims of working with mothers, that is to address children's needs, unless they first respond to the mother's own needs. Survivors Counselling Projects have moved in the direction that Women's Therapy Centres have long recognized, that it is of limited value to provide therapeutic services that simply address the presenting problem, in this case surviving child abuse. A point is reached when a woman moves beyond the label and counselling or therapy considers wider issues for her as a woman. In Women's Therapy Centres and Survivors Projects this will be marked by the boundary between short- and long-term counselling. Initially a woman will be offered a short, time-limited counselling service which will focus on issues around the child sexual abuse. After this, the woman can move on to longer term counselling, where sexual abuse will be one issue among many that are explored within the context of her experience. The major drawback to the provision of this service is the attitude of funders. Increasingly in the 1990s the main funders of women's organizations, that is local authorities, expect miraculously short-term solutions to the difficult situations that women face.

Clearly funders who expect short-term solutions have failed to grasp the depth and extent of the effects of these on women. So, once more, women's experiences are again being minimized and trivialized. There is, moreover, an expectation that counselling will only be offered when there is a 'problem'. 'No problem, no counselling' is essentially the fact of life in the public sector (Dryden *et al.* 1989: 21). A willingness to fund short-term counselling for the woman subjected to the effects of gross sexual abuse as a child is not extended to a willingness to fund the long-term counselling or therapy for the many women who desperately need this. Political and financial expediency becomes the priority and women's needs are denied accordingly.

To illustrate this point, I refer here to an example of a Women's Counselling Project in a Family Service Unit, in an area where this was the only specialist project in the locality. This project was run down over a period of months in 1992, after being in existence for five years. The process started with a requirement from the funders, Social Services, that the service should be limited to counselling women who were mothers experiencing difficulties with their

children, and that the content of counselling should be confined to
these difficulties. In itself this requirement demonstrates a quite
remarkable lack of knowledge and sophistication. The local management committee refused to back the woman counsellor running
the project, who was attempting to find further funding to keep the
project in its original form. Indeed the committee, in the name of
good financial management, further reduced funding. Earlier the
Unit had been granted funds to carry out a research project on male
sex offenders, given because of their proven record in counselling
women. When the Women's Project was reduced, the Unit was in
the position of offering help to male abusers while withdrawing its
previous service to women.

Which activity?

How are the boundaries kept between psychotherapy, counselling,
and the use of counselling skills? As I noted in Chapter 2 these are
not easily drawn but early on in their existence, organizations decided which were broadly appropriate for them. Home-Start and
Women's Aid, for example, are both very clear that the women
who work for them are *not* counsellors, but are workers who
employ counselling skills. Survivors projects and Rape Crisis are
counselling projects where formal counselling takes place. Family
Centres offer counselling as well as other forms of help, such as
advice giving and looking after children. The boundary between
counselling and other activities is marked by rituals, for example,
'We are moving to a special room now, and must not be disturbed
for about an hour . . .'. Women's Therapy Centres, Birmingham
for example, decided that either they will only offer long-term
therapeutic help in the form of psychotherapy, or if they do offer
counselling they have to work out what distinguishes one from the
other. They also have to assess whether counselling or psychotherapy is more appropriate. A Women's Therapy Centre offering
both will have a rigorous assessment procedure covering history,
family situation, presenting problem, current situation, and other
agencies involved. Women for whom therapy is appropriate are
those who have the capacity to reflect on their own part in situations; who are able to make links between the present and the past;
who have sufficient external support to be able to bear the turmoil
of therapy. It is felt that the therapy service should be of a high
standard. In offering short-term counselling for specific problems
and situations for women who do not need or want long-term help,
it is felt that the counselling becomes a boundary for the therapy.

By limiting counselling to a short-term, specific response it is possible to keep the boundary between it and therapy very clear. Other projects which offer long-term counselling find it much more difficult to identify what distinguishes it from therapy, but may not necessarily view this as problematic. They are less concerned about the distinction, and allow the ebb and flow between the two modes in a rather more relaxed way.

Referral of clients

Referrals to women's organizations are usually by phone or letter, although women can refer themselves to Women's Aid or community-based Family Centres. In fact, Women's Aid and Rape Crisis both encourage self-referrals. Whilst Women's Therapy Centres and Survivors Counselling Projects might encourage self-referrals, they are also likely to receive referrals from other professionals, psychiatrists, GPs, social workers, and probation officers. Referrals to Home-Start are mainly from agencies, notably Social Services and health visitors.

Women's Aid, Rape Crisis, and Survivors Projects recognize that some women referring themselves might not want to disclose their names or details about their situation on first contact. The use of telephone counselling skills is vital in these agencies. For women who are highly ambivalent about making contact, this first telephone conversation will be the deciding factor in whether or not they use the agency. Sometimes this telephone conversation will be the only contact they have.

Home-Start organizers take referrals and then visit families for an assessment. If the family wants Home-Start involvement, the organizer matches family with volunteer, based on her knowledge of the volunteers and her assessment of the family. Women's Therapy Centres, Survivors Projects, and Rape Crisis Centres respect the client's right to choose her counsellor. For example, where possible a woman's choice of a lesbian or black counsellor is complied with. Essentially these projects believe that women have rights in the process. In Family Centres choice is made even more directly by the woman herself choosing who she feels she would be comfortable working with. As all workers are trained a client is able to choose freely.

COUNSELLING MODELS

In this section I describe the counselling models referred to in Chapter 2 in more detail. Although there is no uniformity in the choice and use of models, several stand out because of their relevance in counselling women. Writers from Women's Therapy Centres have explored and greatly added to our understanding of the application of psychodynamic models to women's therapy (Eichenbaum and Orbach 1983; Ernst and Maguire 1987; Woodward 1988). While there is considerable variation in the use of models in Survivors Projects, there are commonalities such as the belief that women are experts in their own healing process and that the responsibility for abuse lies with abusers. Some find that the Egan model fits in with a Feminist approach (Hall and Lloyd 1989: 240). Some feel that Gestalt techniques are useful when working with the aftermath of trauma such as rape, violence and childhood abuse. For counsellors in many women's organizations, Person-centred models have been very influential. Underlying the use of these models is the influence of Feminist theories which have informed ways of understanding women's psychological development and of situations which women are subject to because of their social position.

Psychodynamic models

Women's Therapy Centres consistently offer women a way of working therapeutically which is psychodynamically-based. Fewer counsellors working in Women's Counselling Projects use this model exclusively, although it is influential in informing their understanding of both client and counselling process. The early psychodynamic theorists (Freud, Jung, Adler, Klein, Bowlby, Winnicott) were inevitably influenced by the times and culture in which they grew up and their ideas need to be adapted to the present day. Many therapists working in Women's Therapy Centres have been 'drawn to what is loosely called the British Object Relations School and especially the work of Fairbairn, Winnicott and Guntrip' (Eichenbaum and Orbach 1983: 13). This emphasizes the mother–child relationship in the first two years of a child's life, which is seen as the most important for the development of personality. This crucial relationship has been analysed by such women writers as Dinnerstein (1978), and Chodorow (1978: 211) who points out that

> women's mothering perpetuates itself through social, structurally induced psychological mechanisms. Women come to mother because they have been mothered by women.

For Feminist orientated therapists, the Object-Relations approach points to the importance of social experience in human life. Culture too is recognized as of the utmost importance in shaping the psychological development of people: 'femininity and masculinity are psychological entities within a social context' (Eichenbaum and Orbach 1983: 25).

A psychodynamic way of working assumes that a woman's past experiences, particularly early in her life, influences what is happening to her in the present. Understanding these past experiences and how they affect present functioning is seen as integral to the therapeutic process. Counselling or therapy is more likely to be long-term although short-term dynamic approaches exist. These involve working with the transference relationship, that is the relationship between the woman and her counsellor as it reflects other past and present relationships as well as the woman's inner world. Transference refers to the belief that 'in the relationship style(s) which the client adopts towards the counsellor there are signs of past relationships' (Jacobs 1986: 6). Clients *transfer* feelings, thoughts and fantasies about very early relationships on to the counsellor and psychodynamic therapy attempts to identify, acknowledge and work with these during the process of therapy. The transference relationship of particular importance is that which originates from the woman's mother and father. A difficult question that arises for *women* therapists working with women is to what extent they can identify and incorporate the father transference. Freud felt unable to work with the mother transference: he clearly failed to recognize it:

> In 'The Dissolution of the Oedipus Complex' Freud made it clear that he was more confident writing about male children. In attempting to describe the corresponding development in girls the material for some incomprehensible reason becomes far more obscure and full of gaps. Freud later gave as his reason for this that as a male analyst he was provided with less transference evidence than his female colleagues.
>
> (Jacobs 1986: 53)

A psychodynamic model of counselling is one way of exploring how a woman's position in society and her culture affects her sense of self from very early on in her life (Eichenbaum and Orbach 1983: 22). In exploring early family relationships, the importance of these in shaping child and the adult is apparent. Most families reflect the cultural expectations, rewards, affections and restrictions that influence women's behaviour, attitudes and images of themselves as little girls and subsequently as adults. This brief description cannot do justice to the complexities of either female psychological development or Feminist psychotherapy. A useful introduction to such ideas is contained in Eichenbaum and Orbach (1983).

The Egan model

Since the publication in Britain in 1976 of *The Skilled Helper*, the counselling model of Gerard Egan is one that some practitioners find helpful (Inskipp and Johns 1984). The Egan model is a sensitive use of a range of counselling skills in response to a client's needs. This takes place in the context of a caring relationship in which the counsellor can both support and challenge her client. It is a three stage model, of exploration, understanding, and action, identifying appropriate skills for each stage. The first stage is one of exploration and clarification of the problem situation brought by the client to counselling. As the counsellor responds to the client in an accepting and empathic way, she is enabled to explore her feelings, thoughts, behaviour and experiences which relate to the problem situation. In the second stage – greater understanding – the client is helped to see themes, patterns, and broader issues as well as to develop new perspectives about herself and her situation. In the third stage – that of designing and implementing action – the counsellor aims to help the client change in some way, making use of her understanding of herself and her situation.

Many counsellors working with women survivors of childhood abuse, who seek a model which incorporates coping strategies for their client's symptoms, believe Egan's to be appropriate because of its emphasis on the importance of exploring a problem or situation and understanding it, before moving on to action or change. Also it emphasizes the importance of building and maintaining a relationship with the client in order to facilitate this process (Hall and Lloyd 1989: 240–2). Often for women abused as children, the ability to engage in the counselling relationship is the most difficult issue. For many, the ability to trust another person has been destroyed by childhood experiences and building a relationship where there is sufficient trust to facilitate the healing process cannot be hurried. For some women the counselling relationship stands out as one in which they may be able to trust another woman.

Many aspects of counselling women require counsellors to have great self-awareness and understanding, and they will need to examine their own attitudes, beliefs and feelings towards these. For example, the sexual abuse of children evokes powerful reactions in all of us, for different reasons. Counsellors may well have their own history of childhood abuse and issues about this must be addressed and resolved in some way before counselling other women. When working with childhood abuse and making use of the Egan model, the second stage of self awareness and understanding applies at least equally, if not more so, to the counsellor as well as the client. In counselling women, the Egan model is appropriate in any situation where change is desired, and where some form of action or behavioural or attitudinal change is to be implemented. Strategies for coping with depression or eating disorders are good examples of these.

Gestalt model

After training in the 1920s, Fritz and Laura Perls later went on to develop Gestalt therapy. In Britain from the early 1970s onwards there has been an increased interest in Gestalt therapy (Page 1984: 180–202). It is based on an holistic view of the person. No one is seen as inherently good or bad: she is who she is and how she is, making the best of her capabilities at a particular time and in a particular situation. The present is emphasized: people experience, respond, feel and think in the present, in the 'here and now'. In the present interaction between client and therapist, all that needs to be known about a client's history is available. The style of therapy is an active rather than a passive one: the therapist is at ease with emotional expression and intimacy. If required, therapists will make use of techniques and exercises to aid the client in her expression of emotion. Perhaps the two most widely known techniques are those of 'punching cushions' as a way of releasing anger, and the 'two chair' technique.

The two chair technique

The client is asked to move back and forth between two chairs. The chairs can represent a conflict or unresolved situation between herself and another, or they may represent different parts of herself. Seated in one chair she will speak as herself to the other person, moving to the other chair she will speak as the other person back to herself, thus creating a conversation or dialogue.

Counsellors working with women who have experienced trauma, such as rape or childhood abuse, or who wish to explore problematic relationships, present or past, find using Gestalt techniques particularly valuable. Dissociation is a frequent response to trauma. The woman cannot get in touch with her feelings as she has split off or dissociated from them. It is as if they are not part of her. A therapy that is active on occasions and where the therapist is open, encouraging of and comfortable with the expression of powerful emotions, can be instrumental in aiding women become less split off from their own emotions. In Gestalt therapy clients are given permission to express strong emotions. Inevitably women who have been raped or abused experience very powerful feelings. Being given permission to express them suggests to her that in this situation such emotions are normal. In addition, because of social conditioning, women are expected to express some emotions more easily than others. Many women find it particularly difficult to express anger, since socially it is more acceptable for women to cry than to be angry. Again, being offered techniques such as punching cushions, which allows women to express anger towards the rapist or abuser, is seen by some as a potentially liberating experience. As with all techniques, they should not be imposed upon the woman – she must be able to say *no* if she is at all uncomfortable with the idea.

The 'two chair' technique can be used when working with sexually abused women. In the exercise the woman can confront her abuser or another person who failed to protect her. In using both chairs in the exercise she can identify the experiences of the person who failed to protect her. The technique is also used to help the woman confront parts of herself. For example women who experience pain, which is psychologically rather than physically based, may become that pain and explore its function in their lives. In the same way a woman can engage in dialogue with someone in relationship with her.

When working with Polly this technique was used in a most moving way. Polly's mother died of cancer when she was four and she had been brought up by her father. Polly felt that the explanation given her of her mother's death was unsatisfactory. She felt a desperate need, as the four-year old, to ask her mother why she had left her. By using this exercise Polly was able to ask her mother this question, and later by 'becoming' her mother, sitting in the mother's chair, she was given an explanation which included her mother's feelings of sadness at having to leave her daughter.

Person-centred model

The theories of Dr Carl Rogers, the founder of Person-Centered counselling 'percolated spasmodically into Britain in the post war years' (Thorne 1984: 105). During the 1960s his ideas were taken up more seriously and have greatly influenced the development of counselling. Counsellors working in a person-centred way assume that both they and their clients are trustworthy and unique. Counsellors show 'unconditional positive regard' towards their clients. The quality of the relationship between client and counsellor is of the utmost importance. A primary goal for the person-centred counsellor is to see, feel and experience the world of the client as it is seen, felt and experienced by her. The counsellor believes that she will be able to enter the client's world by making an emotional commitment to the client in which she (the counsellor) is willing to show herself as a person with strengths and weaknesses.

Home-Start and Women's Aid, which use counselling skills, have been much influenced by this approach. It also represents the basis for counselling rape victims, sufferers from childhood abuse, and of working transculturally. Person-centred attitudes, of respect and belief in the client's uniqueness, goodness, and trustworthyness are very powerful when women are counselling women. Women's experience in society is that frequently they are discounted and disregarded because of their gender, class, age, and/or colour of their skin. In particular, women subjected to violence as adults or children have not received positive messages but have been treated as objects to be used for another's purposes.

COLLUSION OR CO-OPERATION?

The advantages for women clients working with women counsellors are considerable, and have been a major factor in the establishment of the organizations examined in this book. However, it is important to recognize that disadvantages and difficulties also exist. There is the potential for collusion between counsellor and client, with the counsellor being so in sympathy with the woman that she over-identifies. Clearly, there can be gains in having shared experiences, but these can be unhelpful if the counsellor becomes too enmeshed and loses her ability also to stand back from the experience. There is a danger that both women may sink into depression together, or agree that 'we are all powerless', when faced with issues which are disempowering or repressive. If what the woman describes is too near the counsellor's experience, for instance of struggling with eating disorders, this can be problematic for the counsellor if she has not reached a sufficient degree of resolution herself.

Women working with women can reinforce the stereotype that it is women who are the primary nurturers and carers and that this is inevitably their role. Conversely, however, it is arguable that this role is legitimate and that counselling as an activity validates it in a way unusual in this society. Counsellors need to be aware that clients who particularly wish to explore this aspect of their selves and lives may find it difficult to do so in a situation that re-creates the issues they bring. Once more, a converse argument is available: it is that the very re-creation of the situation provides the opportunity for it to be explored and worked with. An additional dilemma is that caring can be over-emphasized, and negative aspects avoided or denied. Clients may feel protective towards women counsellors, and fear damaging them by relating horrendous incidents or by becoming angry towards them. In a similar way counsellors may be over protective and in their concern not to be another repressive person who does not listen, the therapeutic pendulum can swing the other way so that appropriate challenges are not made. This is a particular issue for those working with approaches that stress the positive sides of a person. It is important that women are also able to acknowledge with one another the negative and difficult aspects of their own selves as well as of the wider world.

Further, issues of competitiveness and power exist for women too and it is possible that these will be ignored by client and counsellor. Women are traditionally not encouraged to be either competitive or powerful, and it can be hard to acknowledge that these issues exist within the counselling relationship. They are of crucial importance when considering the implications of women working with women: without awareness they become entrenched to the detriment of the counselling. This is not to say that this therapeutic pairing is not enormously rich and beneficial. It is important, though, that women are able honestly to acknowledge the potential pitfalls and work with them. This can be a deeply enriching experience for both concerned as they explore together these aspects of women's relationships, and often this will be the first time the client has done so.

SELECTION OF COUNSELLORS

Methods of selection and requirements of women who will become counsellors or use counselling skills vary widely within the organizations. Women's Therapy Centres advertise vacant posts for therapists, often to work on a part-time or sessional basis, and select from a range of candidates who possess the required qualifications in psychotherapy. Family Centres and Women's Counselling Projects within Family Service Units will expect that staff, for example, social workers or nursery staff, either already have a counselling qualification or they will be assisted in gaining one. Home-Start and Rape

Crisis advertise for volunteer counsellors and potential volunteers undertake their own in-house training programme with selection on completion. Women's Aid, in choosing women to train in counselling skills, use criteria based on personal attitudes and attributes, rather than formal qualifications. They believe that insisting on formal qualifications discriminates against women who have been unable to gain qualifications because of their particular life experiences.

Both Home-Start volunteers and Rape Crisis counsellors commit themselves to initial training programmes of about three months. These include sessions in counselling skills, and consistent modelling of these skills by trainers throughout the training. Once selected they will take part in supervision, support groups and on-going training. It can be a requirement that volunteers have experienced the same as the woman with whom they are working, for instance all Home-Start volunteers are parents. Rape Crisis counsellors may have been raped or subject to sexual assault, although others can be accepted. It is felt that working with other women who have been raped may be one way for a potential counsellor to deal with her own experience of sexual violence and it is recognized that other means of resolution should be sought. Therefore Rape Crisis Centres generally have a policy that before being accepted on to training programmes women should have their own counselling if they have been raped. This policy addresses the issue that most hinders the counselling process, that of selecting as counsellors women who are immersed in their own experiences of rape.

Women's Counselling Projects which use volunteer counsellors may have their own training programme or they can select women from local counselling courses as volunteer counsellors in return for expert supervision. Women's Therapy Centres in London and Leeds run their own psychotherapy courses where the emphasis is usually on 'women working with women'. These are one or two year part-time courses, run for women working in outside agencies who have their own clients. Sometimes students will work with clients of the Women's Therapy Centre, becoming their trainees. These courses are in great demand and can be accredited by a local university. For example, the Leeds course 'Working with Women: A Feminist Psychodynamic Approach', is validated by Leeds Metropolitan University at Master's Degree level.

SUPERVISION OF COUNSELLORS

Counsellors working in women's organizations recognize the importance of supervision: conversely, funders are not convinced of its value and are unlikely to finance external supervision. This is particularly the case where funding comes from a Health Authority or a Social Services Department. Their attitude arises from the different requirements for the supervision of counsellors from other staff employed directly by them.

Three main processes and functions of supervision have been identified (Hawkins and Shohet 1989: 41–54), the educative, supportive, and managerial. The educative function concerns the development of skills, understanding and abilities in the supervisees. The supportive recognizes and responds to the ways supervisees themselves are affected by issues, for example the distress of their clients. The managerial function provides the quality control aspect of supervision. If the supervisor is also the line manager, she carries the responsibility that work standards are upheld. At times this function may conflict with the other two. For this reason, some professional organizations, for example the Association of Student Counsellors, require that their accredited members are externally supervised. Supervision of Health Authority and Social Services staff places a great deal of emphasis on the last function, the managerial. The British Association for Counselling state in their Code of Ethics and Practice for the Supervision of Counsellors (BAC: 1988) that:

> The primary purpose of supervision is to ensure that the counsellor is addressing the needs of the client.

and that:

> Supervision is therefore not primarily concerned with:
> (a) training
> (b) personal counselling of the counsellor
> (c) line management.

This is in contrast to the Social Services view of supervision.

Although the educative function may be acknowledged it is unlikely that there is any recognition of the personal effect on staff of this work. This emphasis on the managerial aspect means that the model the funding bodies use is one of internal supervision: a notion of external supervision might appear unusual and unnecessary and is insufficiently understood.

Counsellors place more emphasis on the educative and supportive functions of supervision, and they value the expertise gained from supervision from outside their agency or organization. Therapists in a Women's Therapy Centre have a structure of both internal and peer group supervision but also value external supervision, paid for by the Centre. Counselling Projects and Family Centre workers similarly recognize the need for external supervision and consultation, and prioritize this by paying for it with money they have earned themselves, running courses or providing student social work placements.

Supervisors will be chosen on the basis of their theoretical orientation, their work experience and their personal qualities. Therapists working in a Women's Therapy Centre require supervisors who work within a Feminist psychodynamic model. Counsellors working in other organizations will choose supervisors experienced in their particular ways of working, for example Gestalt or Egan practitioners, or who have expertise, for example, in counselling survivors of childhood abuse. Counsellors working across cultures and within certain cultures might look for expertise in the issues that black clients bring to counselling.

Additionally it is essential that supervisors have experience of working in women's organizations, and some consider this the most important factor. There is also an emphasis on who and how the supervisor is as a woman. Women feel solidarity with others who *know* what it is like to work in women's organizations as well as sharing the experience of being women in this society. Women supervising women counsellors working with women need to explore ways of supervising which reflect the nature of the work. The characteristics of such supervision are explored in Chapter 4.

GENDER, CLASS AND CULTURE

Some women's organizations discussed in this book are pioneers in addressing issues of gender, class and culture. In the mid 1970s, and still in the 1990s, there is a real concern that counselling is a service for white, articulate, middle class clients who can pay for it. Making Women's Therapy Centres and other women's organizations accessible reflects a powerfully held conviction that women from different classes and cultures should feel welcome and comfortable in using the services, and should do so regardless of income and status.

Writers, notably from the London Women's Therapy Centre (Eichenbaum and Orbach 1983; Ernst and Maguire 1987), have been the forerunners in actively considering issues around gender in therapy and counselling. Women's Aid and Rape Crisis both understand the experiences of the women they work with in the context of their role in society. As each project is autonomous, the way in which this belief is translated into practice varies from project to project, also reflecting the range of Feminist beliefs and values as well as crucial common ground. How this is expressed in practice is relevant to clients who sometimes feel that services are too political or too dogmatic. For example, a woman who has been raped often experiences a multiplicity of confused and complex feelings. Her perception of Rape Crisis Centres as holding a clear-cut view can conflict with her own confusion and lack of clarity.

Some organizations emphasize gender issues whilst others emphasize culture. Home-Start and Family Service Units are examples of those that emphasize culture and racism. The initial training programme for Home-Start volunteers includes sessions on working with parents from different cultures and on racism awareness. Training relating to gender issues is not undertaken. Although some Home-Start organizers see themselves as Feminist, training that specifically relates to women's place in society and the effect on mothering is limited. In the same way, in Family Service Units, with its emphasis on culture and race issues, issues of gender can be overlooked.

It is very difficult for organizations to maintain an appropriate balance between gender and race issues without ignoring or minimizing either. Even within one organization, workers can hold opposing views, as illustrated by two black women counsellors from Family Service Units. One stated that:

> 'women speak a universal language. It is more important that women work with women, culture is a secondary consideration. Women have the common experience of being oppressed.'

The other's point of view was that:

> 'women are from the same culture first, being women is a secondary consideration. Women cannot fully understand women from another culture or who are a different colour.'

This inevitably means that whenever culture is considered the more important, women's issues take second place.

Less thought is given in these organizations to issues and implications of class and age. My example, in Chapter 2, of ageism and cushions may be appropriate here. The woman in question felt really upset and unwanted. In their consideration of different cultures, the effects on women of the cultural differences between classes within Britain is rarely explored. The question relating to potential differences in counselling working class women and middle class women seems studiously ignored. As more is written about working with women from different social classes (Butler and Wintram 1991: 44–70), it is important that this filters through to women's organizations. This point is explored more fully in Chapter 6.

The issue remains of providing counselling services for both young (that is mid and late teens) and elderly women. Clinical experience indicates that elderly women (65 and older) make less use of counselling services than younger women. If accessibility to women's organizations is to be taken seriously it is important that efforts are made to develop a service relevant to elderly women. The reasons they do not currently use counselling services are complicated. As a generation their upbringing did not encourage exploration of feelings and desires, and so counselling becomes an alien activity. For different reasons services for very young women are limited. Without a specific identity, for example as a mother or an abused woman, they do not fit into the existing ethos. Women's Therapy Centres do provide a therapeutic service for *all* women. However, probably because their therapeutic work tends to be long-term, it may mean that many very young women find it inappropriate. At their particular age therapeutic work lasting for a year or two might appear extremely daunting.

This chapter has considered how issues in counselling particularly relate to services for women. It is essential that those involved in practice, training and supervision in any context where women work with women have considerable awareness of these issues and their implications. Questions relating to boundaries, accessibility of services, the appropriateness of the setting, and many others are pivotal if counselling is to be effective, appropriate and a real response to the needs of women. In writing this chapter I am again impressed by the commitment and energy shown by workers at all levels in actively exploring these areas. Their desire to offer women services of the highest standard, in a climate that does not support them either financially or emotionally, is a measure of their belief in their work.

· FOUR ·

Specific issues in counselling women

Throughout the agencies, a characteristic feature of women's organizations is their cohesiveness. For example, Home-Start includes counselling skills training as part of its volunteer training programme, and active listening in particular is emphasized throughout. All involved are expected to incorporate listening skills into the ongoing process of learning. In the same way, organizers engaged in interactions with volunteers will be using these skills, both in individual and group contexts, and in supervision. Family Centres, set up specifically to provide counselling, require all staff and volunteers to be adequately and appropriately trained. This includes secretarial and reception staff who are valued as front-line workers; therefore training is beneficial both in their day-to-day contacts with parents and helps their fuller understanding of the work undertaken.

Women's Therapy Centres, Rape Crisis Centres and Women's Aid, stress the importance of their organizational style so that it reflects the content of the work. As I referred to in Chapter 2, issues of power and hierarchy are considered in organizational terms. When so much of counselling women centres on themes such as low self-esteem and difficulties in self-nurturing, it is vital that the services they use are seen both to care for their workers and encourage their self-esteem. This philosophy is reflected in the provision of adequate supervision and individual support, and by encouraging the possibility of counselling for staff.

AGENCY TRAINING

Home-Start, Rape Crisis, and Women's Aid provide their own local training programmes for volunteers. Women's Aid additionally offer regional and national training including counselling skills in their programmes. Importance is also placed on on-going training days which volunteers are expected to attend. For example, a day on 'Further Counselling Skills', perhaps led by local Relate trainers, will build on the foundations already laid in the initial programme. Traditionally local Marriage Guidance Councils (Relate) provided counselling skills training for voluntary and statutory agencies and in the past were one of the few agencies where such training might be bought in (Dryden and Thorne 1991: 3). Nowadays, this picture is changing rapidly, and the growth of counselling courses now provides a wealth of similar resources.

Basic training programmes for agencies should include the counselling skills of listening, empathizing, clarification and challenging. These are identifiable skills to be learnt and practised, and used by the worker in obtaining information, clarifying problems and facilitating decision making. Women are frequently empowered by the discovery that they have already been using these instinctively, although without defining them. Personal qualities of the trainee are equally necessary: warmth, approachability, empathy, acceptance of others, respect for others, open-mindedness, flexibility, non-dominance and objectivity are all important (Scottish Women's Aid 1991: 11).

Training programmes should include information about local resources. Organizations which do not offer counselling to women need to know for referral purposes where this can be obtained. Trainees need to assess when counselling is appropriate and to be familiar with referral procedures. For example, training programmes could explore the effects of bereavement and relationship dynamics, enabling appropriate referrals to agencies such as Cruse and Relate.

Women's issues

Training programmes also include specialized knowledge relevant to the work of the agency. For example, sessions may cover aspects of mothering and the effect of depression on women. Particular questions may be emphasized, for instance the high incidence of depression amongst isolated working class mothers of young children. The effects of domestic violence and sexual abuse, including rape and the effects on adults of childhood sexual abuse, need to be explored. On-going training days examine areas especially relevant to counselling women, such as teaching assertiveness skills or

information about eating disorders. The prevalence of eating disorders amongst women illustrates the importance of such training:

> up to 20% of normal women binge eat once a month, 90%
> have been on slimming diets and 10% have used vomiting
> and laxative abuse as a method of dieting at some time. In fact
> disordered eating behaviour and attitudes are so common that
> as a woman you are abnormal if you do not follow diets and
> worry about your weight. Concerns about the body and self-
> image are intricately woven into being a woman.
>
> (Dolan and Gitzinger 1991: 1)

Continuing training also gives opportunities for increasing self-
awareness, viewed as essential if this work is to be undertaken
properly. Rape Crisis counsellors are actively involved in counselling rape victims, and self-awareness is essential both in initial and
longer term training. The opportunity to reflect on yourself, and
how you are affected by the content of the work, is also built into
support groups and supervision. For Home-Start and Women's Aid
befrienders who are not actually counselling, the need for self-
awareness sessions is not so great, but is still a consideration. These
helpers inevitably hear some horrific detail and need help in coping
with this. Horrifying stories can be recounted unexpectedly. One
Home-Start volunteer recounted how in her very first visit to a
young mother, she listened to the woman's story of the gross sexual
violence perpetrated on her only the night before. This story took
two and a half hours to tell. The effects on the young mother were
appalling. But the effects on the volunteer were also considerable.

OUT OF AGENCY TRAINING

Many agencies which either employ staff as counsellors or run
volunteer counsellor schemes will expect or encourage their counsellors to take up external training. Some services offer psychotherapy in addition to counselling, although the distinction between the
two may not always be either clear or significant to clients. Women's
Therapy Centres employ women who are qualified psychotherapists
and whatever the emphasis of training, Women's Therapy Centres
work with a Feminist psychodynamic framework. Styles vary as do
the ways in which various Feminist ideologies are applied to therapy
(Chaplin 1988a: 39). This is explored further in Chapter 6.

Family Centres, Rape Crisis, and Women's Counselling Projects are likely to expect that workers have had some prior counselling training. Inevitably, potential workers will be drawn to locally based training courses which have a particular theoretical base and students will be influenced by those. However, these agencies believe it is useful for staff to have a working knowledge of a variety of theoretical approaches. Of course, counsellors themselves will be attracted to models of counselling that suit them and make sense to them, particularly if as clients a certain approach has been helpful.

Counsellors working with women very often find that they are creative in their use of therapeutic techniques, flexibly incorporating different aspects from a range of approaches. Women will be able to juggle ways of working, reflecting their skill in juggling competing demands more generally in their lives. This is illustrated by the way different theoretical orientations merge and blend comfortably together in counselling in women's organizations. Beliefs, attitudes and techniques are taken from different theories relevant to women's lives and experience, joining together creatively into their own unique model. There is no need for the rigidity that so easily occurs when models are uncritically absorbed, which characterizes many male-dominated services in the mental health field.

Many workers strongly emphasize humanistic ways of working. Women are viewed as innately good having within them their own potential for growth. They are recognized as being in charge of their own healing process. These beliefs and responses are very powerful offering a radically different model to women. This approach is highly relevant when counselling in a cross-cultural context. It emphasizes similarities rather than differences between people, and underlines the belief in equality between client and counsellor. It is therefore appropriate for counsellors wishing to work in a universalist rather than a separatist way.

I referred in Chapter 2 to the significance of the psychodynamic approach, the backbone to the Women's Therapy Centres approach. This has been far reaching in its influence on working with women, and many counsellors who are not psychodynamic practitioners recognize and acknowledge insights and understanding thereby gained, which they have incorporated into their own practice.

A range of approaches are recognized as relevant when working with women. For example, Gestalt techniques (see Chapter 3), assertiveness training and 'Inner Child' therapy (Parks 1990), are often used when working with women subject to abuse, whether it is domestic violence, rape, or childhood abuse. 'Inner Child' therapy believes that:

Inside every adult who was sexually abused are the feelings of
the little girl she once was. That little girl is still frightened,
confused and crying – waiting to be comforted by parents
who will never come for her . . . That child needs to be comforted, needs information about what has happened to her
. . . Until the 'child' is comforted, the 'adult' may not be able
to take the governing role in her life.

(Parks 1990: 48)

Techniques from a cognitive restructuring framework may be
appropriate when working with women who are depressed. Nairne
and Smith (1984: 159) comment that:

this is a form of therapy developed by Aaron Beck, rather
specifically to help people who are depressed. The theory is
that depression is caused by certain thoughts, attitudes and
ways of viewing the world. A cognitive therapist will help you
to identify the pessimistic and self-derogatory thoughts which
lead to your depression and will teach you to substitute more
positive thoughts. This is obviously not as simple as it sounds
and has to be worked at over a period of time.

Behavioural programmes from sex therapy treatment, for example female self-focusing or sexual assertiveness (Gillan 1987:
167–87), are used when helping women explore issues of sexuality.
Body-work is also of value when exploring female sexuality, assisting women in knowing and enjoying their bodies as they are, rather
than in the ideally stereotypical images so beloved by the media.
Whereas some counsellors, for example those from Rape Crisis, will
have a foundation of Feminist ideology underlying their counselling
models, others such as those from Family Centres or Family Service
Units, use an integrated model appropriate for women, but will not
necessarily define themselves as Feminist.

Case illustration

In this case illustration, although I have changed the client's name,
another has been chosen to illustrate the point. Bobbie's counselling illustrates an integrative model in action. She was a twenty-five
year old mother of an energetic three-year old son Ryan, and she
sought help from a Family Centre. She had a history of emotional
and physical abuse in childhood and had had three periods of
psychiatric in-patient care for depression. She enjoyed her unusual
name, applicable to either sex, and on occasions her appearance
demonstrated its masculine alternative. The choice of name reflected

her mother's wish for a son and the parental neglect was partly because of her gender. Bobbie's physical appearance frequently changed, reflecting her mood swings, and was often an odd, sometimes bizarre, mix of masculine and feminine.

Her counselling lasted for approximately a year and a half. During that time Bobbie was introduced to and practised cognitive restructuring techniques as coping strategies for the depression. There was an emphasis on Gestalt techniques, which facilitated conversations between the different parts of herself, particularly the masculine and feminine parts of herself about which she felt so ambivalent. That is, she was taught always to look for the positive in her achievements, rather than blame herself for what she perceived as failures. Thus, when she said 'yesterday I wasted loads of time because I was feeling so awful. I felt so bad that Ryan was affected. I told him off so much I had to take him to the park in the afternoon, to make up for it', this was reframed as 'despite feeling so low yesterday, I managed to take Ryan to the park in the afternoon. He really enjoyed himself.'

Gestalt techniques, such as the 'two chair' exercise, proved to be a useful way of focusing on and exploring this ambivalence. Over many sessions, Bobbie came to see the importance of both sides of her and how the positive sides of each were a source of strength. She was also able to 'own' the female part of her, so discounted by her parents. Lastly there was an emphasis on, and exploration of, the relationship that developed between Bobbie and her counsellor. As Bobbie's experiences of being mothered were not 'good enough', the counseling relationship took on aspects of a 'restorative re-mothering'. Chaplin (1988b: 38) cautions that:

> Many therapists today prefer to talk about re-parenting or about unconditional positive regard, in which the therapist is seen as re-parenting the client, through unconditional acceptance. These words do not have quite the same numinous symbolic power as does the word 'mother', but we can be on dangerous territory if we use the term 'mothering' without stressing the differences between the symbolic meaning of the word and actual human beings who mother. It is also vital to talk about mothering as essentially a function, not a thing, not static. It is one aspect of all human relationships. It is a particular kind of relating, one that is generally understood in our society.

Organizations that are responsible for their own training need to incorporate and acknowledge the relevance of different theories, although they may emphasize one more than others. Skills need to be taught alongside theories and some will also offer specific modules on issues for women in therapy and other concerns, notably cross-cultural counselling. Sessions which explore the roles of other professionals, for example psychiatrists, psychologists and social workers, and consider appropriate referrals, are important to include. These individuals and agencies are of considerable value and ensure that accurate information is available to common service users.

A major issue for workers becoming students, is the degree to which they are subsidized for the training. Women's organizations committed to working with trained counsellors may well decide to assist with the cost. Without such assistance many, but particularly working class women and those from ethnic minority groups, may be discouraged from becoming students (Dryden and Thorne 1991: 13). An essential element of all aspects of these agencies is the recognition of reality factors in women's lives. This must be reflected in the availability and the cost of training, if these philosophies and beliefs are to be effectively translated into action.

SPECIALIZED KNOWLEDGE

In counselling women some issues are so frequently presented that specialized knowledge is essential. Knowledge relating to the effects of childhood abuse and violence in adulthood is one key area. These effects are long-term and extensive, touching most areas of a woman's life. Self-destructive behaviour can result, manifesting itself in many ways – suicide attempts, slashing or cutting her body, or setting up situations which are guaranteed to fail. This self harm arises from a deep sense of worthlessness, despair and rage. The little abused child has no choice but to feel that there is something wrong with *her*, if she is being treated in such a way. There is no other way such a small person can make sense of her appalling treatment. She is too young and too oppressed by the abuse to understand that the responsibility lies with the abuser. Frequently a woman subject to domestic violence or rape encounters very clear implications that she has invited or caused the violence in some way. Abuse as a child leads to adult inability to trust, with implications for all her relationships, whether these are with lovers, partners, children or her counsellor. The experience of violence at any age creates trauma and counsellors need to be aware of its effects. Details may need to be recounted again and again before they can be resolved, or dissociation can be apparent, experienced as a psychological distance between the person and others.

Eating disorders

Eating disorders are a major issue for women. We saw earlier in the chapter that their prevalence is so great that for white western women they are almost the norm. Anorexia (not eating), bulimia (binge eating accompanied by forced vomiting or excessive use of laxatives) and over-eating, are aspects of many women's lives. Although men are also affected, there is a much higher incidence among women: the ratio of men to women is placed somewhere between 5 per cent (1 in 20) and 10 per cent (1 in 10) (Bryant-Waugh 1991: 75).

To understand this phenomenon, the social expectations on women with respect to food have to be appreciated. Women have a long history of being responsible for feeding others. Today it is women who mostly buy and prepare food for partners and families. What and how it is prepared might indicate both their social status and their effectiveness as a wife or mother. Yet women are also expected to be very careful about what they eat. The social expectation of slimness is very powerful and thus food becomes an area of conflict and contradictions for women. Over-eating, to the extent of causing massive weight gain, is one way women feel they can either protect themselves or somehow be treated with respect, as 'weighty' individuals. Additionally over-eating may occur either when women are not in tune with their bodies, or when extremely uncomfortable feelings are experienced and these can be temporarily extinguished by constant nibbling. Consuming food is not straight forward for many women. If the complexities of eating, illustrated by the following quotations, and the symbolic nature of food are not understood, these difficulties can only be inadequately addressed.

> Fat is a social disease. Fat is about protection, sex, nurturance, strength, boundaries, mothering, substance, assertion and rage. It is a response to the inequality of the sexes. Fat expresses experiences of women today in ways that are seldom examined and even more seldom treated . . . What is it about the social position of women that leads them to respond to it by getting fat?
>
> (Orbach 1978: 18)

and,

> Is it a coincidence that the 'thinness ideal' developed with the emancipation of women in the west? The more women aspire to equality of social status the more society despises the female body with its natural fat deposits, curves and roundness.

We are asked to deny our womanhood and our adult status
as a sexual, fertile adult, to hate our fat and curves, and to
exchange it for an ideal which is similar to the shape of pre-
pubertal child or man. Are women exchanging the bondage of
one body shape for the enslavement of another?

(Dolan and Gitzinger 1991: 5)

Depression in women

Similarly counsellors will need to understand the nature of depression experienced by women if they are to offer effective help. The
higher incidence of depression among women results from a number
of factors. First, hormonal changes resulting from the pattern of a
woman's reproductive life are relevant (Ashurst and Hall 1989: 19–
26). The depression which can result is exacerbated by patriarchal
attitudes which, instead of accepting and celebrating such biological
differences, imply that women's bodies are inferior. Second the
dreariness and drudgery experienced by mothers of young children
needs to be fully appreciated. Moreover the way that women are
treated on a daily basis as if they are of little value, is another
important factor that is sometimes conveniently minimized. They
may become depressed when relationships break down through
divorce or death, or when children become independent. Women
are defined by their relationships; they take responsibility for them,
and the impact of failure is immense. The loss of babies, whether
by cot death, still-birth or miscarriage, is often catastrophic, although
recognized as such only very recently. Others present as depressed
when in reality it is their partner who feels this way.

Women often carry the depression within the relationship
and express feelings for both partners. This arrangement saves
many men from getting depressed: their wives do it for them.
It is not in the interests of such men that their wives should
cease to be depressed, for that might mean that the man has
to own his own depression.

(Rowe 1991: 174)

Another factor not always sufficiently understood is that women
are socially expected not to express feelings of anger or aggression
– this would not fit with the stereotype of femininity. Anger not
expressed can be turned inwards and become expressed as depression. The depression is intensified if the cause is not identified,
unravelled and resolved. For example, Amy, who is 46, had suffered

periods of depression since her adolescence. As her parents lived abroad, she and her brother had been sent to boarding school in this country from an early age. She described her elderly parents as old-fashioned: any crying, temper tantrums or over excitement were firmly squashed. Her parents' attitudes, combined with loneliness at school, meant that she kept tight control of her feelings, turning them inwards, particularly when angry. As an adult the only mood she could identify was depression.

Sexual orientation and culture

Another key area presented to counsellors are the implications of the woman's sexual orientation, and therefore a knowledge of lesbian as well as heterosexual sexuality is required. Similarly learning about different cultures, and understanding how growing up in a particular culture affects women's lives is of obvious importance, and needs to be a central consideration in a multi-cultural society. The concept of culture is not static – it is changing all the time, and therefore awareness is an on-going process, not a one-off event. Ethnic minority women in Britain struggle both with the demands of their particular culture and the demands from the society in which they grew up and live in. The resulting need for integration of different life styles, attitudes and beliefs is a particularly complex and powerful struggle for women.

Women's psychology

While in-service training should include information about the above issues, an exploration of women's psychology is vital. Innovatory thinking in this area has been developed particularly by women therapists working in Women's Therapy Centres. Study groups examining questions relating to women's psychology were set up early on in the history of the London Women's Therapy Centre (Ernst and Maguire 1987: vi). Meeting each week, these were for staff members of the Centre and drew on their own personal experience, their clinical practice and their reading of Feminist and psychoanalytic work. Again this is another expression of the integrating and valuing of all aspects of a woman's life so central to the philosophy of counselling women. Non-hierarchial study groups discussed and explored women's psychology, a profound and necessary challenge to existing views and theories. They sought to integrate the many strands of theory, clinical practice and their own experience. They developed ideas; they wrote and they published.

Their views were also heard and taken seriously by a wider audience, although simultaneously their work was absorbed into the Centre and its clinical practice.

Women working with women

This exploration and development of women's psychology was and is of great value to women counsellors. However this was not their only achievement. The theme of women working with women, and issues relating to this, was also identified and has been much discussed since. Women counsellors and women clients share the experience of being the same gender in a society that in many ways deems them to be second class citizens. It is important to consider the assumptions they thereby hold in common, and that these are adequately acknowledged in the counselling. As described in Chapter 3, the counsellor can over-identify with her client, and both women can collude over expectations of their caring roles. Moreover it can be hard for the client to accept the care without feeling undermined and the counsellor may experience unconscious, or conscious, feelings of jealousy. She might resent her client being given what she herself needs and would like to be in a situation where this would be available.

Women supervisors

One of the ways women counsellors care for themselves is by recognizing the importance of supervision for their work. How supervisors are chosen is relevant: they are frequently selected for their expertise and how they think, relate and act as women. The characteristics of this three-way dynamic – a woman supervising a woman counselling a woman – are explored by Jewett and Haight (1983: 165), who argue that the feminine style of supervision has characteristics of its own.

> My work was supervised by a woman whose style was indeed feminine: relational, collaborative, collegial. This in no way meant that we did not think about the work, or that it was in any way disorganized – quite the opposite. Quality of work was assured.

The supervisory task is seen by Jewett and Haight (1983: 171) as one of consolidating learning that facilitates the integration of personal and professional functioning in the spirit of collaboration. Supervisor and supervisee work together on the material, rather than the supervisor taking the expert role.

The more important task of supervision is to keep the super-visee in touch with her own internal and external resources for healing both emotional and spiritual. The collegial ap-proach constantly re-emphasizes and demonstrates that the human psyche strives towards wholeness and contains within it the necessary power for its own healing. The supervisor's task is to provide the interpersonal context in which the super-visee can be empowered to heal others.

The image that comes to mind from this passage is that of the midwife, the supervisor assisting and encouraging supervisees as they give birth to their own healing powers.

Women counsellors often choose to see women supervisors and their choice should be respected. They find that open trusting re-lationships are more easily achieved, as the complexities of gender issues, or overtly competitive feelings, do not apply in the same way. The genuineness and respect felt between supervisor and counsellor is also felt for and towards the client, in a way which only happens when the threesome are women. Because all three share the experience of being a woman, there are some dynamics in the relationship which do not have to be spelt out; they are simply and instinctively known. In the supervisory relationship, great feelings of respect for and pride in the achievements of the woman client can be felt by all three: a feeling of solidarity.

A further consideration is that there is less likelihood of sexual exploitation, either through sexual misuse or inappropriate sexual behaviour and remarks. As with the woman counsellor and client, they are likely to feel, and be, safer. Intimate matters, often expressed in the counselling of a woman by a woman, are easier to talk about with a woman supervisor. When these matters are sexual, there are no feelings of voyeurism when explored in supervision. Lastly, even women who are not overtly political are more aware of women's issues so supervisors and counsellors always share some essential common ground. They are also more likely to be aware of the development of women's psychology, and to draw upon, use and integrate their knowledge within supervision.

THE STRESSES OF COUNSELLING IN WOMEN'S ORGANIZATIONS

The stresses encountered by women who counsel within women's organizations are many but can be be grouped into three main areas. First, those relating to issues external to the agency, including

working and communicating with other agencies. Second, those
involved in working within the agency itself, and third, those arising from the work content, and how the woman worker is affected
by these.

External factors

A major cause for concern for most of the organizations covered in
this book is that of under-resourcing by their main funders. Workers
have to become more involved in fund raising activity themselves,
and may even have to raise money for their own posts, for example
as has happened in some Family Service Units. Some workers are
shielded from direct financial stress as their organizations have co-
ordinators or managers responsible for fund raising. However those
which work as a collective or a non-hierarchical team are deeply
affected by such concerns.

Another major stress is the large and increasing numbers of referrals. Potentially, and often actually, there is too much work. In
part this is due to organizational success, although public awareness
of issues such as domestic violence and rape, and knowledge of
resources are other factors. All the services discussed in this book
have been inundated by women disclosing childhood sexual abuse.
This has been a growing trend since the mid 1980s when the high
prevalence of sexual abuse within families began to be identified,
enabling women to disclose their abuse, with the hope that they
would now be heard and believed. For many this was not so previously. Increase in referrals also reflects lack of other counselling
provision for women. Services that offer this find that there is no-
where else to refer women, even if they feel other help would be
more appropriate. For example, the Leeds Women's Therapy Centre
finds that because of a lack of other counselling and mental health
provision, women referred to them are more disturbed than previously. These clients are taken on, but it is recognized that they are
time consuming; for instance liaison with medical staff is necessary.
Although ultimately the Centre knows such therapeutic work can
be successful, the funders' framework for success may be different.
They may want a rapid through-put of clients, thereby identifying
success in terms of numbers, whereas the counsellor may view this
in terms of the client's diminishing need for psychiatric care. Para-
doxically, this may mean that although the client takes more time
from the Centre, overall less is taken from other services. However
funders may choose not to share this understanding, thereby im-
posing a further strain on staff.

In a similar way liaising with other agencies is stressful when they do not sufficiently understand the nature of the work. A Women's Aid worker might have to educate others, for example, police, health workers, social services, about domestic violence and its effects if they are unaware of these issues. Other agencies may or may not welcome this education, but if it is not undertaken, unrealistic expectations of how women behave and feel in these situations can lead to very inappropriate interventions.

Internal factors

As previously discussed, in some organizations counselling is one activity among many, and workers can find managing different roles containing inherent conflicts difficult. Even finding a quiet space in the midst of the creative noise and activity of a busy Family Centre or Women's Aid Hostel is a major achievement in itself. Those organizations whose main funder is Social Services do not place a high priority on women's need for individual counselling when their main focus is child protection. Gender issues can be insufficiently acknowledged when issues of race are emphasized, and all too often it is seen as a choice; either issues of gender or issues of race are highlighted. Yet both contribute to, and are relevant in, any serious consideration of oppression and oppressive experiences, and both must be held constantly in view. Neither should be lost because of the other. Defending counselling provision for women in an agency which emphasizes its child protection function and which has discarded consideration of gender issues because of its concentration on issues of culture and racism, requires enormous energy. There is a danger that equal opportunities procedures are so powerfully emphasized that concentration on racism becomes an exclusive ideology, gender issues are forgotten, and little is done to tackle all the underlying factors in oppression.

Effects on individual workers

The biggest stress on women workers is the content of their work. Day after day they hear details of the most horrific experiences that happen to human beings. Working with domestic violence, rape, and the experiences of survivors of any type of childhood abuse, is working at the 'heavy end' of counselling. Being continually exposed to repeated stories of violence, can in itself be experienced as abusive. Whereas other professional workers can more easily build defences against such such stories, women involved in counselling need to remain open and accessible to their clients and are therefore more vulnerable.

Many involved in counselling will have experienced themselves the horrors they hear from others. That is, they will have been beaten, raped, or subjected to childhood abuse. If this is disclosed on applying to be a volunteer counsellor, their acceptance may be delayed until they have themselves received sufficient help. However such memories are often repressed and hidden from consciousness and are triggered by counselling a woman with a similar history and story to tell (Perry 1989).

Effects on women in their relationships

Little has been written about the effects on counsellors of the content of their work or on how this affects their relationships, although reference is made to the effects working with sexual abuse has on helpers (Perry 1992: 77). Moira Walker (1992: 195) includes discussion of this in her book *Surviving Secrets*. She suggests that

> The personal relationships in which the therapist is involved can be affected in many ways. It is a considerable bonus for a helper to be in a loving relationship which is supportive and understanding, but stresses can be imposed upon the strongest of relationships. Both partners should be aware of this possibility and should understand something of the cause of such stresses. Continually hearing details of abuse makes the most trustworthy relationship open to question and doubt: the helper begins to feel that nothing is ever what it seems. Sexual difficulties can arise, especially if the helper is working with clients disclosing details of sexual abuse.

Women counselling women become starkly aware of the oppressive nature of social relationships and the potential for oppression in relationships between women and men. Time and again in supervision women counsellors tell how their relationships with male partners are affected, if only temporarily, as this example illustrates. Hilary is a counsellor in a specialist counselling project within a family centre.

> 'Listening to so much abuse of women or even just about the drudgery of women's lives, affects me at home sometimes. I find myself looking at Simon and thinking "would you ever treat women like this, what are you capable of?". If this

crosses my mind, then I have to stop myself thinking like that. Our sexual relationship is affected – I'm not so interested in sex at times. I get preoccupied with details of the childhood sexual abuse I've heard. When that happens I have to make a big effort to switch off from it.'

Counsellors report that relationships with other males in their families are affected. With growing sons, thoughts similar to those Hilary had about her husband can occur. Women find the gender issues normally present between themselves and sons in early adolescence are exaggerated or that the emergence of male sexuality in the same age group seems more difficult to accept. Inevitably working or training as a counsellor creates ripples in immediate relationships. Indeed, some counselling training information carries warning notices of the likely effects on the student's family (Leicester Relate 1992). Women counsellors working with women, whether or not they are subject to violence, become increasingly aware of gender issues, both generally within society and specifically as manifested within their family relationships. The other relationships immediately affected are those between mothers and daughters. These relationships are a particularly significant and absorbing theme in counselling women. Since the mother–daughter relationship is crucial to an understanding of women's psychological development, the counsellor cannot remain unaffected by consideration of this issue, particularly as, for some clients, re-mothering is an important aspect of the counselling process. Counsellors may feel that they never stop 'mothering', both at work and at home, and have to take care not to become depleted.

Women counsellors need to consider seriously the extent to which they should erect firm boundaries between their work and their family lives. All counsellors value the walk or drive home from work to create distance from it. For those involved in intensive counselling, either in terms of numbers seen or subject matter encountered, the journey home might not be sufficient. The need and desire for time and space for themselves when they arrive home is unlikely to be forthcoming. Most mothers are aware of the barrage of practical and emotional demands that will be put on them as soon as they step over the threshold. Demands also exist for fathers, especially those of young children, but the difference for mothers is that they feel themselves to be, and others see themselves as being, responsible for emotional support. They work with relationships all day and come home to be faced with even more emotional demands.

SATISFACTIONS

The list of satisfactions for counsellors is not as long as the one of stresses. Yet what it lacks in quantity it makes up for in quality! When counsellors in women's organizations talk about their work, and the opportunity it provides to facilitate another woman's growth and development, they do so enthusiastically. It is a powerful experience to be with women as they grow in self-confidence, esteem and self worth as a result of counselling. It is the other side of the coin of identifying with another woman's experience of oppression. Sharing the experience of being women in a society which discriminates against them is, on the one hand, a source of stress for counsellors, and on the other an enormous satisfaction. Being at the birth of another woman's growth of confidence, assertiveness and independence, which enables her to make real choices in how she wishes to live, is so pleasing precisely *because* both client and counsellor experience oppression. The feeling of solidarity, alluded to earlier, is part of the satisfaction. I have referred in several places to the large number of women presenting with a history of abuse and other experiences of violence. It is a privilege to be part of a process where remarkable changes can take place for them.

There is a transformation in women during counselling, and a transformation in their lives, that goes on before the counsellor's eyes. It is difficult to convey sufficiently how enriching it is to see the woman, who initially was so oppressed and frightened that she cowered in the waiting room or was unable to talk to the receptionist, develop into an upright, self-confident woman. Women counsellors welcome and celebrate the opportunity to counteract, through the quality of their relationships with women, these oppressive childhood and adult experiences.

Experiences as volunteers

I include the experience of being a volunteer in my list of satisfactions. While there may be difficulties in the role I would essentially view it as a very positive experience, and it is certainly a feature of a number of the organizations I describe. Becoming a volunteer gives access to training and this can enable many to start re-entry to education that they had never considered possible. It brings the satisfaction of belonging to a dynamic and highly supportive group. The growth of self-confidence and self-esteem seen in women clients is equally true for women volunteers, some of whom have been clients themselves. Of course, the experience of volunteer work is not straightforward. There can be difficulties and drawbacks as well as gains.

'The stress of being a volunteer is that you can do *too* much and therefore become ineffectual and so leave the scheme. Therefore you do need to take the support of the organizer and the scheme and we need to have careful care of that. The satisfactions that are around, I think are a great deal. You have the satisfaction of belonging to a scheme which does support you well, which puts on good training, which has good social events and which carries quite a lot of clout and status in volunteering and also gives you an opportunity to explore yourself, to learn new things and to move out and on from here.'

(Home-Start organizer)

The stresses and satisfactions for these women often reflect different facets of the same issue. Counsellors live in the same society as their clients, face similar issues and are subject to the same discrimination. Much of what they hear is painfully familiar to the counsellor, but this is balanced by the enormous satisfaction of empowering women, through counselling, to be who they want to be. Although the stresses are easy to identify and list, they must not obscure the energy and optimism of women who have worked in these organizations for many years, They are a testimony to the commitment of these groups and point to the deep satisfaction that can be gained by women working with women.

· FIVE ·

Professional relationships in counselling for women

WORK WITH VOLUNTEERS

In Chapter 4 I looked at the satisfactions of being a volunteer in organizations, either as a counsellor or as a befriender. This chapter extends the discussion into an exploration and examination of the relationship between professional and volunteer. Some schemes, such as Rape Crisis and the Asian Women's Counselling Service, are established as volunteer projects with one or two organizers involved in training, support and supervision. Others make more limited use of volunteers and their inclusion in a scheme is likely to present some problems.

One volunteer's experience illustrates the teething troubles of setting up a women's counselling service staffed by volunteers within the social work agency, Family Service Units.

> 'At the beginning I was treated with what I can only call polite suspicion by staff – not so much by the administrative staff but certainly by the social workers. I remember on my second visit being followed round by one social worker to make sure I could have no access to confidential material. Of course I understood his concern, but I did feel rather as if I was from another planet.'

Although the volunteer experienced a degree of wariness by all members of staff, there was a vast range of different responses. First there was the concern that outsiders would now have access to confidential material. This concern is entirely correct. However the social worker seems to have put little trust in his female colleague in charge of the scheme, to raise the issue of confidentiality with the volunteer either at selection or during supervision. Linked to this were concerns about the degree of responsibility that volunteers might expect to exercise, and whether they would provide a professional service.

Interestingly, one female social worker did give a very positive response to the scheme. She herself had trained in social work after being a volunteer at a Family Centre while her children were small, in the way outlined in Chapter 3. Many more women than men are volunteers as it fits more easily into women's work and life patterns and they are more likely than men to understand the demands and commitments involved. For many women it is a route into further education or professional qualifications. A further anxiety relates to the potential political implications of using volunteers. This can adversely affect funding since funders can argue that providing professional services is not economically justifiable when volunteers appear to do the same at much less cost. To return to my example and as is often the way, in time the volunteer came to be regarded as an invaluable part of the social work service and thus eased the way for other volunteers who later joined her. Her experiences were similar to those of other women pioneers who have to prove their capabilities to a sceptical world.

This particular example also illustrates the ambivalence of the social work profession towards volunteers and this has a long history. Whereas other professionals, for example in education or health authority settings, have a more ready appreciation of the work of volunteers, this ambivalence is partly due to the struggle of social work to achieve and maintain professional status. Particularly over the last two decades it has become increasingly difficult for social workers to maintain their belief in their professionalism. This has been hard hit by both public sector financial cuts and the bad publicity relating to child protection cases. Consequently confidence has been greatly eroded. There is a resulting, and understandable, fear that volunteers will undermine the profession even further. Additionally men predominate in social services management and they do not easily appreciate the use of volunteers, while women regard this activity with far less suspicion.

When volunteers are accepted as a valuable resource, considerable time and effort has to be put into their support. Rape Crisis Centres make much use of volunteer counsellors and know that for this to be successful funding for volunteer organizers has to be made available. As shown in Chapter 4, Home-Start organizers are aware that their job of supporting volunteers is vital in order to prevent 'burn-out' and therefore to minimize the loss of those in paid jobs within the organization. Working with volunteers, in terms

of support, supervision and training, is time consuming and is a
major reason for organizations not wanting to use them. Effort has
to be spent to ensure that volunteers find their work suitably re-
warding. Since voluntary work attracts no financial reward, a sense
of achievement in being of service, or satisfaction in working for a
cause one believes in, or the intellectual stimulation gained, must
be sufficient recompense.

Great care has to be taken not to exploit volunteers. In the early
stages, trainee counsellors with access to expertise and stimulating
supervision, find that the rewards for volunteering are sufficient. As
time continues and with some training and experience, the question of satisfactory rewards again needs to be addressed. One consideration is whether the organization itself provided the training in
which case trainees may be expected to 'pay back' the cost of this
in terms of work. Others who fund their own training and undertake voluntary counselling to gain experience and fulfil their wish
to help, can be open to organizational abuse and misuse by being
used as cheap labour.

This situation arises partly because of the current state of counselling training. Unlike other professional training, for example of
teachers, doctors and social workers each with their own nationally
agreed standards, counselling training standards can be set by individual organizations and training bodies. Inevitably there will be
variations, confusion and lack of clarity. The question arises whether
training within one organization, for example Rape Crisis, qualifies
the counsellor for work in another, or whether it is organization-
specific and so not transferable.

There is a large pool of counsellors working in a voluntary capacity
in many organizations. An overwhelming proportion of these are
married women (Dryden *et al.* 1989: 15). This poses a very difficult
dilemma for women organizers. The organization may need more
staff when the demand for counselling is high, and frequently the
only available response is to use more volunteers:

> 'We use volunteers a lot here. In fact I've been trying to
> organize longer opening hours so we could use even more. I
> make sure the training is good and that there is a good sup--
> port network. I also monitor what work they take. Many of
> them are local mums, and it's a good way for them to be still
> involved. I always encourage them to apply for jobs as well.
> They get a lot out of being a volunteer but its only a stepping
> stone.'
>
> (Family Centre organizer)

This particular organizer sees her task as providing quality train-ing and support for volunteers. She also views their work as an important but temporary step towards other employment. However not all volunteers are used in this responsible way. One solution to the dilemma of a volunteer being inappropriately used, or in-adequately trained and supported, is to provide her with a clear contract stating the training offered and agreeing the length of time worked in return. On completion, she would be helped to move on, or the contract can be re-negotiated. This ensures through-put of volunteers and reassessment of their role. However this raises the question of how many volunteer counsellors can actually move on to alternative occupations. There is also the possibility that some will not wish to, and may prefer to remain in a voluntary capacity. Perhaps what is important is that which ever system is used, it should offer flexibility while protecting the interests of the volun-teers. Another solution is to pay experienced volunteers sessional rates for their work. This also has to be undertaken with care. It is problematic in any organization when some volunteers are paid and others are not. The rationale for this needs to be clearly speci-fied and understood and accepted by all concerned. Where this is felt appropriate, agencies raise money, or earn it by offering training for this purpose, and often involve experienced volunteers in this process.

Another difficulty relates to volunteers who are appointed but are found to be lacking in competence. In this situation it would clearly be unethical to allow the volunteer to progress further, but the dilemma is not straightforward as the following account by one organizer explains:

'I learnt the hard way. At the beginning of the scheme we had one volunteer who, after a few months, did not seem to be gaining insight either in what was happening for her clients or to herself. She had a qualification in counselling but this was her first experience of practice. It got rather nasty as there was no procedure for "dismissing" a volunteer. I instituted a six month trial period after that. When a new volunteer starts it is made clear that the first six months are a probationary period and only at the review stage will someone be accepted.'

However when it works well there are enormous satisfactions in providing opportunities for volunteers to develop and change. They become increasingly confident and assertive and this is energizing and encouraging for other staff members. Many continue into fur-ther study and professional training, particularly within the field of

social services. For instance, it is not uncommon for the volunteer
helper in a Family Centre to have been a parent customer herself,
who then goes on to undertake social work training.

RELATIONSHIPS WITH OTHER PROFESSIONALS

When a counselling service for women is one aspect of an organization's function, it takes place in a context where the predominant
professional outlook is likely to be different. There are considerable
implications and many potential conflicts of ideology when counselling occurs in a setting predominantly geared either to social
work or education. For instance, in Social Services, the service will
have been conceived for mothers rather than all women. Its existence
will therefore be justified by emphasizing better care for children.
In this way counselling may be expected to centre around child
behaviour management or around the mother–child relationship.
Referrals will be made within this schema and will have identified
the need for counselling in terms of child protection. There will also
be an expectation that counselling will be short-term.

The following example of a referral to Family Service Units by
Social Services is a common one. A social worker referred a young
mother aged 24 with three children under four. She was described
as possessing an uncontrollable temper, and the social worker re-
quested that counselling help be given to control this, particularly
in respect of how it affected her children.

In this way the social worker had identified the problem, had
decided what was necessary, and had thereby defined the focus and
task of counselling. Since his primary task was child protection, he
assumed that this would also be reflected in the counselling process.
From the outset the counsellor was faced with an assessment, in
which neither she nor the client took part, by another professional
who clearly had no understanding of counselling. The counsellor's
assessment was very different:

> 'The client was certainly very angry, but then she had a lot to
> be angry about in her life. In my contract with her, she wanted
> to explore the reasons for her anger, to have it acknowledged,
> and to be able to express it appropriately rather than extin-
> guish it. There seemed little point in trying anger manage-
> ment techniques – the social worker had already tried these
> and it had not been helpful. Social workers often refer to us
> with the idea that if we do precisely what they have already

tried, somehow it will work this time, which is rather like shouting louder and louder at a foreigner in the hope that they will understand.'

The relationship between counsellors and social workers is coloured by their different expectations, assumptions, and understanding of counselling, as this example clearly illustrates. As in this case, counsellors have to justify a service, where women clients control the process and where issues are not simply related to mothering; this is seen as only one aspect of their lives. Further, funders expect services to concentrate on mothers, raising the question of where women who are not mothers receive help, unfortunately implying that women are only important because of their children and not for themselves. Women seen for counselling within a social work agency will be treated differently from those using other services. Difficulties and tensions ensue with counsellors having to justify their work and others resenting it as an unnecessary luxury. Avoidance of central issues results, dialogue between counsellors and social workers safely centres on administrative detail, and the clash of philosophy is denied. Of necessity the counselling service frequently has a waiting list whereas other workers, with their different ethos, can quickly offer initial appointments and rapidly assess both mothering skills and the risk of possible child abuse. Their waiting list is clearly prioritized in these terms whereas their counselling colleagues prioritize on a different basis that is not understood. Counselling services have to justify waiting lists in a context where a rapid turnover of clients is valued and often demanded. One project described how their funders, Social Services, expected their service for adult survivors of childhood abuse to achieve its aims in six sessions, an expectation echoed by other organizations. This is clearly ludicrous, but illustrates vividly both the lack of understanding from those in charge of funding, and the enormous pressure applied to those already stressed and pressurized by a demanding job. Funders can demand that a service focuses on specific groups. For example, the Leeds Women's Therapy Centre, funded by Social Services, is expected to cater for particular groups, in this instance women who grew up in care and mothers of sexually abused children. As I indicated in Chapter 2, this Women's Therapy Centre responded by providing a short-term counselling and groupwork service for these women. If longer term work is needed it is offered, and other aspects of their lives will then be addressed. The power of funders is considerable and obvious, and creates moral and professional dilemmas for those responsible for service

provision. They are frequently left with no option than to be sta-
tistically 'creative', and selective with the truth. In this way they
walk a tightrope, keeping funders happy whilst attempting to protect professional standards and to offer appropriate help to the
women they care for.

Social Services are not the only agency to make life difficult in
this way. Other referral agencies also feel they have a right to dic-
tate what are, and are not, acceptable and significant areas of a
woman's life. This is not helped by the lack of sufficient knowledge
from other professionals about the particular context of the service
being offered. One example is domestic violence:

> 'One of the biggest problems for us is working with other
> workers, such as the police or social services. They invariably
> have no idea of the degree of support a woman needs nor
> do they understand the complexities for women in violent
> relationships.'
>
> (Woman's Aid worker)

Again there is a need for consistent dialogue between the women's
organization and other professionals. Information about the nature
of counselling and the situations that women are so frequently in,
needs to be given. However this also has to be taken seriously by
the professionals who so often have the power, but without having
the necessary knowledge to use it correctly.

Organizations also need to address the question of their potential
misuse in another way. It is important that unsuitable referrals are
refused, and that they are not used simply for those problems which
other agencies do not want or cannot handle. Women who need
help not available elsewhere can be referred to counselling as a last
resort, and women's organizations thereby become the 'dustbin' for
other agencies. It is horribly easy to become trapped in this role, as
it can feel very callous to refuse services to women when nothing
else is available. A further scenario is when it is clear to the counsellor that the client would benefit by being offered help from her
organization, and yet this has to be refused since its primary function
is differently defined and decided elsewhere. This is compounded
by the expectations of other agencies and of the women workers
themselves. The very prevalent and stereotypical attitude that women
take on everything, put others first, do not complain, is insidious
and it colours other people's views of women's organizations. Male-
dominated agencies, such as Social Services, have a central ethos in
which goals are set and efficiency, rapid turnover, and gate-keeping,
are stressed. There is an inbuilt assumption that other agencies

should work similarly and accept their ethos as correct. They are not able to see that other styles are different, and not inferior, and they do not pause to consider the relative validity of differing approaches. These rigid pervasive attitudes make it essential for women's organizations to be clear about boundaries relating to referral and assessment procedures. They also regard efficiency as essential, but their way of achieving this takes a different, less rigid route. When refusal of a referral is appropriate, it should not be accepted because of these external pressures.

Lastly there is a complicated dynamic in the relationship between counsellors and their professional colleagues. Other workers often envy counsellors. Counselling is an activity in which change and transformation of people is possible, both requiring and engendering optimism in attitude and outlook. Other professional activity, such as social work or teaching, may well effect change, but the process is different. Generally, those who use counselling do so as a very positive choice, as do those entering some, but not all, levels of education. However this is rarely so for Social Services where a policing role is so apparent.

Carole Sturdy, exploring the susceptibility to envy of psychotherapists working in Women's Therapy Centres, looks at their relations with clients as well as other professionals:

> They are, therefore, likely to be vulnerable to the envy of their clients. Psychotherapy professionals are, perhaps, particularly vulnerable in this way, not only in relation to users, but also to others in the caring professions and who, because they feel themselves to be working under considerable pressure and stress, are envious of the working conditions they see therapists enjoying, the time and thought they can give to their clients.
>
> (Ernst and Maguire 1987: 41)

This envy can manifest itself in different ways. Counsellors can be treated with anything from wariness and scepticism to downright hostility by other professionals. A frequently expressed feeling is that 'counselling is easy', it does not concern itself with 'really difficult' cases as, by implication, do the other professionals. The woman counsellor can be left feeling as if hers is not 'real work', an echo of how 'women's work' is not socially valued and respected. The reality does not reflect this fantasy. As this book has shown, women who counsel women are faced with levels of pain and agony often avoided by other agencies.

RELATIONSHIPS WITH MALE WORKERS

Many of the organizations covered in this book are women-only projects. Family Service Units are likely to employ as many men as women workers, whereas Family Centres and Home-Start are likely to employ a few men. A major difference is that Family Service Units are likely to be managed by men, whereas Family Centres and Home-Start will have women managers. It would be simplistic to suggest that all women managers support women's issues and facilitate the growth of services which will empower women users, and all male managers do not. Some women's counselling services have been well supported by male managers. However when re-sources are limited and funding is reduced, or when it is granted by male-dominated agencies, only the most committed and aware of men will run against the tide and fully support counselling provi-sion for women.

Women counsellors relating to male colleagues who represent the funding agency, are negotiating with a representative of a male-dominated culture. Butler and Wintram (1991: 173) describe this experience:

> The oppressive position in which women are placed in patriarchal agencies is reinforced by the expectations of us, which are so much higher than for men. On the one hand we are expected to conform to professional and agency codes of conduct which bear little resemblance to our experience. On the other hand we have to be more intelligent, more efficient, more malleable than male colleagues. The getting by, the complacency, that men are permitted, is never allowed us. Behaviour which is tolerated from men damages us and others all the time. Double standards definitely prevail.

The struggle to defend a counselling service for women, or nego-tiate funds, when such forces and prejudices exist, is enormous. This is particularly difficult when women are struggling against male organizational culture when those involved are not aware of its repressive nature. However lack of male awareness in this situation is frequently accompanied by a defence of the ethos they uncon-sciously represent. It is ironic that Social Services Departments care-fully implement equal opportunities policies and anti-discriminatory practice while doing nothing to analyse the sexism inherent and deeply ingrained in their structures. Both the structure and culture of Social Services is reflected in their attitudes to funding: women are neatly categorized as if the problem becomes manageable by so doing.

Certain problem categories are generalized which become shorthand ways of reducing women's pain to manageable proportions. These categories also reinforce prejudicial statements about women.

(Butler and Wintram 1991: 34)

Women thereby become labelled as 'inadequate', depressed', 'deprived', 'immature', 'potential child-abuser', and many more. Women counsellors who challenge and confront the non-acceptability of this process find themselves part of it and are themselves labelled as 'difficult', 'unreasonable', 'naive', 'not living in the real world', or are accused of lacking objectivity and becoming over emotional and too involved. This is, of course, a method of invalidating women and their views that has a very long history in this patriarchal society. It creates an effective double-bind. Whatever women do, think or say, is turned back against them as a proof of male superiority and female incompetence and foolishness. It reveals a sexism which leaves neither the woman client nor the worker any room for negotiation. In male-dominated agencies little value is placed on either women workers or clients. When these attitudes prevail, services for women have very great difficulty in surviving in any meaningful way and their work is neither recognized, acknowledged nor valued.

In contrast are many hope-giving examples where women and men work fruitfully and sensitively together to offer services for women. Pen Green Family Centre employs a woman manager and male social workers and some male nursery nurses. They are available to counsel, so women users of the Centre have a choice of gender of their counsellor. A man and a woman co-lead a long term therapeutic group for women survivors of childhood abuse. This co-leadership model was deliberately chosen, carefully thought through and has run for a number of years. It was felt important that different male behaviour was modelled to group members who had previously often experienced only repressive and abusive treatment by men. The male leader needs to be gentle, non-intrusive, and sensitive to women's needs, treating them as people and not objectifying them. His existence as a group leader allows members the opportunity to work with and through their ambivalent attitudes towards men. Women counsellors who choose to co-lead groups in such a way recognize the need for on-going open analysis of their relationship although this can be both challenging and demanding, but they feel the advantages of such a co-leadership model outweigh the difficulties.

RELATIONS WITH OTHER ORGANIZATIONAL
WORKERS

The tensions that arise between workers in the same organization centre mainly on issues arising from structural factors, but may include difficulties about differences of approach. Surprisingly perhaps, differences sometimes emerge after success stories. An example from Home-Start illustrates this point. After successful Home-Start involvement, a client's sense of self-esteem was so improved that she was able to find paid employment, which necessitated her making nursery provision for her children. However while some workers would perceive this as a very positive indication of change, others would have misgivings about helping women who then decide that they do not want to look after their children on a full-time basis themselves. The volunteer befriender's aim is to help women look after their children in the best possible way. When she is faced with the decision that some women take that their best way is employment for them and care for their children elsewhere, a conflict results.

In one sense differing attitudes are positive: they provide the basis for ongoing debate, but they can also be threatening and challenging to the workers involved. The fact that these conflicts arise reflects the ethos of the organization which clearly carries the danger that women become stereotyped; 'good mothers' are only those who stay at home. Such a view is in conflict with an aim of Home-Start, that of essentially meeting the needs of mothers as women who can then more fully respond to their children. Value judgements about the nature of good mothering undermine such an aim. A further difficulty in accepting a view, that suggests that women can go to work and also be good mothers, is that it challenges an essential aspect of the organization, that it depends on 'good mothers who stay at home' for its volunteer labour force.

ORGANIZATIONAL STRUCTURE

A major issue is whether or not the organizational structure facilitates and reflects the nature of the work undertaken in the project. The structure inevitably influences relationships between workers. Some projects will be organized as collectives with a Feminist perspective which is reflected both in the types of task undertaken and also in how these are carried out. Collectives require enormous energy from the workers in order to maintain such a structure.

Carole Sturdy, writing of the London Women's Therapy Centre, illustrates this:

> during the three years that I have worked as an administra-tive worker, the group has been engaged more or less ex-plicitly in a process of defining, sometimes re-defining, its overall aims and objectives as an organization. Sometimes this process has felt like questioning an inscrutable sphinx, trying to decipher her riddles and at the same time learning to tolerate the anxiety or dread which such a state of uncer-tainty generates.
>
> (Ernst and Maguire 1987: 31)

The creation and maintenance of this process takes time, energy and commitment. Some larger projects find it too time consum-ing and after much deliberation they decide to establish a manage-ment structure which separates policy making from the actual work. Smaller projects can work in this congruent manner because they are managed either by one woman, or by two operating a job-share. Job-sharing works very effectively when the two workers know each other well, are confident and positive about their relationship, and allow themselves sufficient 'hand-over' time. Counsellors working in a project where counselling is one function among many often wish that they could organize and control their working environment so that it more readily reflects the nature of the work taking place. The greater the individual's involvement in counselling, especially where the content is emotionally demand-ing, the greater the need for quiet, time for reflection, and time to recharge the self. Working with deep emotions depletes the coun-sellor, and considerable energy is required to replenish her own emotional resources. To do this, she must have control over her environment, impossible in a busy and noisy Family Centre or Family Service Unit. Locating counselling activity in a wing of a building or a suite of rooms helps considerably.

In the example of the London Women's Therapy Centre we see the epitome of emphasis on process. By this I mean concentrating on all aspects of the organization's operation; how the service is provided, how it evolves, how workers relate to each other, as well as the work itself. To put this in group terms, there needs to be emphasis both on maintenance as well as task. Task refers to the work that is done; maintenance to the integrity of the relationship structures which allow the work to be done. Organizations which are male-dominated often emphasize making decisions in as speedy a manner as possible. Women work differently, valuing and using intuition to help them understand the processes they are involved with. As a result female managed organizations adopt a style that is more co-operative and collegial, whilst also being effective and efficient.

These differences in style and approach between women and men can be identified early in child development. Gilligan (1982: 10) cites Piaget's observations that:

> through childhood, boys become increasingly fascinated with the legal elaboration of rules and development of procedures for adjudicating conflicts . . . Girls are more tolerant in their attitudes towards rules, more willing to make exceptions and more easily reconciled to innovations.

Counsellors whose work incorporates an awareness of therapeutic processes can transfer this concept to thinking about organizational issues, but administrative staff need to be introduced to such concepts. Otherwise tensions may arise as administrative staff fail to appreciate the value of time spent in team meetings and other activities that are geared to this way of working. Conflicts and misunderstandings occur in a similar way with male colleagues who operate from a different basis and can often be unsympathetic and threatened by the alternative model.

This is not to suggest that concentration on purely 'female' organization will provide perfect answers. Carole Sturdy in her chapter 'Questioning the Sphinx' (Ernst and Maguire 1987: 30–47) explores a number of ways in which she feels such an approach falls down. She feels, because of their male connotations, there is wariness about 'management' and 'management tasks' that has unhelpful implications for how administrative workers are viewed:

> The group does not recognize management as a necessary skill at all, but as something that anyone can do as a sort of sideline to their real work. It may vaguely be conceived of as running the centre and in practice consist of responding to emergencies as they arise, and generally 'muddling' through. The reluctance to admit the need for management is one cause of the suspicion with which 'admin' is regarded.

She goes on to state that

> anyone taking on a management role, part of which consists in exerting controls, can be seen as the 'enemy within' whose feminist theory becomes suspect.

In this way, women managers face problems of isolation, lack of role models, and little support from other workers. This can occur in female-only groups, although it is more generally recognized when they are in a male-dominated situation. In a research study (Alban-Metcalf and West 1991: 167) of women managers, the vast majority of comments described difficulties arising from being female in a male-dominated organization. Overall there

> was the feeling of isolation at work, of seeming to operate according to principles quite different from male colleagues and a constant feeling of being under close scrutiny and being tested by a suspicious audience who never accepted you as one of them . . . several women expressed their frustration and depression at the lack of support . . . a few felt very strongly the lack of a female role model.

The women managers I met while researching this book did not work directly in male-dominated organizations, but their roles inevitably involved contact with men in senior positions, either as funders or as line managers. Although I met with a range of women certain common characteristics were evident. Their energy and enthusiasm was evident and impressive. They related to colleagues on professional and personal levels; they knew them well both as colleagues and as women in a wider context. They were aware of the need to be flexible and incorporated this flexibility easily; for instance, employees were able to leave early to collect children and it was accepted that they would work equivalent overtime to compensate. This was not regarded as a problem or a weakness in the woman, or in the organization. Rather it was regarded positively and as a strength. Lateral thinking enabled imaginative responses to problems: for example when training or staff counselling was given high priority but funds were not available, pragmatic approaches to raising extra funding were explored and implemented.

There is a need within women's organizations for there to be a balance between 'female' and 'male' ways of operating. Women need to own the 'male' parts of themselves. By this I mean characteristics such as single-mindedness, the ability to compartmentalize, to be able to take ultimate responsibility, to act powerfully; at times all are necessary when exercising management functions. Being powerful and in control is often uncomfortable for women, who so often experience powerlessness and being controlled, and do not wish to impose this on others. Women managers need to learn to incorporate more comfortably these elements into their work in a way that does not destroy or negate their own style of being and organizing. They have to discover that by so doing they do not revert to the very male management style they seek to avoid. By becoming less frightened of exercising power they recognize and forge their own pathway in their own mode. Conflicts may result on occasion, and women managers who feel that it is their responsibility to make relationships work experience anxiety if uneasy relationships result from their managerial decisions. Again they learn with experience that these can be acknowledged and resolved and that conflict is growth-producing and not destructive, if handled carefully and thoughtfully. Decision making is an important part of any managerial role, and discussion and analysis relating to these enables exploration of new ways of working. Carole Sturdy argues for

> the need to reclaim the 'male' aspects of running an organization; in particular the need for management. Perhaps part of differentiation for a woman involves reintegration of the so-called male parts. For those of us who are therapists, dealing with the emotional areas of life is in some ways an extension of the mothering role, as are some (but not all) aspects of administrative work, whereas theorizing about activity for a public audience is more commonly done by men.
>
> (Ernst and Maguire 1987: 6)

RELATIONSHIPS WITH OTHER COUNSELLORS

Women counsellors meet with others outside their own organizations for support and friendship as well as for professional networking in a way that is characteristic of women. They are concerned to reach out and communicate with women counsellors working in other institutions and agencies, such as within Higher Education, Relate, or private practice. Their expectation is that they will have much in common both as women working as counsellors and women working with women clients. These connections operate formally and informally. Women's Therapy Centres, with their provision of courses and workshops formally facilitate and nurture the development of such professional networking. Spontaneous contacts arise between women meeting at conferences who stay in touch and offer one another support not only because their jobs are similar but also because they are attracted to each other as people.

Reactions to counselling services provided by women's organizations are very wide ranging. There is little recognition or acknowledgement of the use made of counselling skills by workers in projects such as Home-Start or Women's Aid. This reflects the way that little is known about the effects of violence or the experiences of mothers with young children. In part this is due to the discounting of women's issues in society generally. Within the counselling community both projects fit into Charles-Edwards's category of community self-help:

> the largest agency within this category is undoubtedly the Samaritans, which has always eschewed the notion of counsellor in favour of that of 'befriender' . . . Characteristic of them all is their commitment to specific causes such as the needs of mothers with pre-school age children . . . The agency is often local, strongly rooted in its immediate community and concerned as much with the provision of services for advice, information and advocacy as with counselling.
>
> (Dryden *et al.* 1989: 16)

Having identified different categories of counselling activity, Charles-Edwards identifies a number of sources of tension within the British Association for Counselling (BAC), the organization representing the whole range of counselling practice. He notes five sources of tension, and three are relevant in this context as reflecting differing and opposing views:

(a) those who are employed as counsellors and those who regard counselling and pastoral care as a central component of their work;
(b) those who are paid for their work, whether by salary or fee, and those who work voluntarily;
(c) those who are radical and have a concern with the social implications of counselling and those who take a more conservative stance by arguing that counselling is concerned with helping the individual to change, not with changing society.

> (Dryden *et al.* 1989: 17)

These account for the insufficient attention given to projects such as Home-Start and Women's Aid. Increasingly the counselling world is becoming hierarchical, with paid counsellors claiming more status and the greater number of volunteer counsellors being given less. Consequently projects fitting the 'community self-help' category are seen as relatively insignificant. Women's Aid and Rape Crisis become victims of the third tension mentioned above: they adopt an appropriately radical stance, and are concerned with the social implications of counselling. Insufficient value is given to the use of

counselling skills when working with women traumatized by violence or who are mothers of young children. Similarly, insufficient
attention has been paid to the quality of the provision of counselling
in many Rape Crisis Centres, although as with Women's Aid, they
are highly significant in bringing the plight of many women into
public awareness.

In contrast, there is another reality. Therapists and writers from
Women's Therapy Centres are rightly seen as the forerunners in
considering issues that women bring to counselling. Surprisingly
little has been written about women's psychological development
and about women in therapy and counselling in the UK. Many of
the publications that have been written are by women working in
or connected with the London Women's Therapy Centre (Goodison
1981; Eichenbaum and Orbach 1983: Ernst and Maguire 1987), or
by women practising as feminist therapists (Chaplin 1988b; Walker
1990). Since little else has been written, these authors come to be
labelled as 'experts', a label which fits uncomfortably with their
therapeutic outlook. The notion of 'expert' and client originates in
the very models these women therapists react against. Jocelyn
Chaplin (1988a: 52) describes this well:

> Just as I encourage the client to develop new kinds of inner
> and outer relationships, so I am concerned to develop differ-
> ent relationships between client and therapist. So my starting
> point is always from a position of equal valuing and respect-
> ing. Inside myself I am aware of my own problems, weak-
> nesses, vulnerabilities. At another time I could be sitting
> in her chair telling her my troubles. But at this particular time
> we have a contract for me to be in the role of therapist and
> for her to be in the role of client. And I certainly do not start
> pouring out my problems to her.

CONCLUSION

This chapter highlights the differences between the cultures of
women's counselling projects and external realities, whilst also
emphasizing the considerable pressure from the wider world to
conform to its patriarchal ways. The projects demonstrate different
ways of viewing clients, different ways of working together, and
different ways of providing services. They are energetic, facilitative,
flowing, evolving and impressive. I visited; and describe here, organizations that are in sharp contrast to the male cultures surrounding them, with their narrow task orientation, stressing goals

of productivity, success and quick results. Communication between the two cultures is, not surprisingly, difficult. However it is ultimately to the benefit of both if dialogue is encouraged and established. Traditional male management models have a huge amount to learn from the more flexible, fluid and co-operative methods preferred by the women I met. It remains to be seen if men are able to consider and incorporate these new and challenging ideas. The threat to established tradition may be too great even if established tradition is often shown to equal ineffective management, lacking humanitarian principle or practice. At the same time, women need confidently and firmly to grasp the male prerogative of power and control, to challenge its negative connotations of intimidation and devaluing, and facilitate its use in a way that can benefit and empower women.

· SIX ·

A critique of counselling for women

Projects which provide a counselling service for women find themselves in a unique position at the present time. Many of them are actively involved in pushing back the frontiers of knowledge about the issues they are responding to and about their client group, in addition to the provision of counselling. Consciousness-raising and the dissemination of knowledge are integral parts of their work. Further, unlike many other counselling agencies, women's organizations are instrumental in thinking not only about the theoretical implications of the counselling they offer but also about *how* it is offered, and about the ways in which organizations are structured and operate so that they reflect the needs of women clients and workers.

The women's groups explored in this book have made a considerable contribution to knowledge about the counselling needs of women. This has ranged from an understanding of how women are affected by eating disorders, depression, or violence to an understanding of issues such as female sexuality and spirituality. They have contributed greatly to knowledge about women's psychological development, pointing to the central importance of the mother–daughter relationship. They have highlighted issues of women working with women and the implications of this for the support and supervision of women counsellors.

THEORETICAL PERSPECTIVES

It is apparent that the theoretical models used in counselling women have been adapted and developed to be relevant to them. Women's

Therapy Centres chose to work within a psychodynamic framework from their inception, whilst other projects have chosen other models in response to changing demands or worker preference. The theoretical stance chosen by the Women's Therapy Centre workers derived from a belief that it offered the opportunity to explore women's psychological development. For example, it allowed them to explore the difficulty and the reasons for women's reactions to the struggles, tensions, and ambivalence inherent in their social roles. Women's Therapy Centre practitioners have been instrumental in the evolution and application of this theory to women.

For other agencies, their counselling model evolved through an interweaving of the response to client issues and the expertise of their workers. An example of this is Pen Green Family Centre which began by training workers in counselling skills using Egan's three-stage model. In responding to adults abused as children, a Gestalt model of counselling was chosen, partly because of the expertise of two of the workers, whereas in counselling depressed women cognitive and personal construct theories and techniques were found effective, both having been suggested by a woman supervisor. Additionally, through her own experiences in therapy, a Pen Green worker had developed an interest in Gestalt methods. At a Rape Crisis Centre, workers expressed their belief that their project as a whole was enhanced by a large number of their counsellors having their own counselling. The importance of this is that women counsellors make use of their own experience and insights in order to measure a model's relevance when working with women: theories are tested as to their validity against women's experience and knowledge. In contrast to other counselling, such testing of theory against experience is acknowledged as an essential feature of the process. Feminist interpretations develop this theme by emphasizing the shared experiences of client and therapist, based as they are on a political critique of women's role in society and an understanding of the effects this has on women's emotional development.

Yet while the choice of model is appropriate to the client group, how appropriate is it for the organization? One difficulty that besets counselling services is that agency expectations, and more particularly those of their funders, are greatly at variance with the counselling needs of women users. While this is a theme in most of the projects examined, it features prominently for Family Centres and Family Service Units. Both agencies are established in urban areas of high deprivation. They are likely to be the only counselling resource so demand for the service is high. Women counsellors

working in such projects recognize the need for a long-term counselling response to the issues women bring to counselling, and en-
deavour to provide this. These resources are particularly important
and significant in that they provide a service for working class
women. This is rarely acknowledged but is remarkable since

> for many working class women the very mention of the word
> therapy can be off-putting, since it is seen as an indulgent,
> navel gazing, soft, middle class activity irrelevant to their lives.
> Some of this antagonism is justified in that a lot of therapy
> shows an inadequate awareness of class issues – the so-called
> bread and butter of poverty, hunger, cold, homelessness, etc.
> and fails to address issues like the cost, language, style and
> assumptions of therapy that effectively exclude most working
> class people. I see some working class criticisms and anta-
> gonisms as buying into the lie that it is unnecessary for us to
> think and reflect on ourselves and how we feel, that it is
> indulgent to take care of ourselves physically, emotionally
> and spiritually.
>
> (Trevithick 1992: 65–6)

Trevithick questions the London Women's Therapy Centre's ability
to overcome the wariness of working class women to therapy. This
further emphasizes and validates the need for Family Centres and
Family Service Units. They are able to be inviting and acceptable to
working class women and their setting within a working class community and as a resource only for members of that community is
a very significant factor.

Since funders, even those with a specified purpose to provide
services for these communities, do not recognize or acknowledge
the importance of such counselling provision, the needs and concerns of working class women are once more overlooked and seen
as less important than those of women from other classes. Also, in
the name of greater efficiency, short-term counselling and a fast
rate of turnover is expected, and counsellors have to justify the
long-term responses that, as I have shown, are needed if effective
responses are to be made.

Although these centres are the only therapeutic resource within
the community for children and families, their primary emphasis is
on children. Women are essentially viewed as mothers by organizers and funders, and so discounted as women. Agencies lose sight
of their function as a community mental health resource when

the focus is so firmly on children, and underestimate the value of a counselling resource for women. It is evident from the high demand that women clients want and need a service that offers long-term help, and women counsellors are prepared and able to provide this. However the power to fund or not belongs to managers and funders, usually men, who are failing to acknowledge the value of the service they choose to curtail. Once again, men are not listening to women.

The seriousness of the situation should not be underestimated. It remains to be seen whether agencies such as Rape Crisis, Women's Aid, and Family Service Units will survive the fate of other voluntary organizations, namely that withdrawal of funding will lead to closure. Both Women's Aid and Rape Crisis have been immensely successful in raising public awareness about the issues surrounding domestic violence and rape. Their careful analysis of violence against women is Feminist in nature, clearly demonstrating this exists as a regrettable and totally unacceptable consequence of the societally defined power relationships between men and women. Both organizations provide a free service to women regardless of class and both exemplify the way women have come together to provide a service to other women where statutory services have been non-existent and disinterested. Having achieved so much in terms of consciousness raising, often under hostile conditions, it would be tragic if they had to close when what they offer is vital and unique in a context of increasing reports of violence against women. If they were to close now, not only would a free service be curtailed but the particular Feminist analysis of violence would be lost or inevitably diluted. If this does occur it unfortunately reinforces the view that it is men who generally take policy decisions and men who choose not to take seriously the difficulties of women although they are intimately involved in their causation. It will be a retrograde step if in the 1990s this view is given greater credance, rather than greater challenge, by the provision of fewer rather than more services for women. Policies that seem intent on demolishing agencies by the simple expedient of removing funding, make a nonsense of apparent notions of 'community care'. The provision of services becomes a meaningless concept, rather than meaningful action. As ever it seems that women are at the bottom of the pile, and inevitably it is working class women who suffer most. What price patriarchy is a question that cannot be avoided. It would be a naive assumption that it is simply accident or coincidence that in times of cutback it is women's services that are hardest hit. At some level – although this may be a mixture of the conscious and the unconscious, the planned and the unintended – this is a deliberate intentional policy.

COUNSELLING SKILLS

Organizations which choose to make use of counselling skills rather than expect their workers to be counsellors, made this choice as an appropriate expression of their organizational aims. Of course in so doing, they are less likely to have to struggle with funders in justifying this particular aspect of their work. Two of the women's projects, Home-Start and Women's Aid, believe the use of counselling skills to be appropriate to their common aim, that of being *alongside* women users. They believe that to have women working as counsellors would interfere with that aim. Thus, Home-Start volunteers are befrienders who need to adhere to more fluid boundaries than counsellors in order to work successfully. For example, if a worker feels it is appropriate to visit a family in crisis three times a week instead of once, then flexibility is needed, whereas counselling with its stricter boundaries would impose too formal a structure on befriending. Women's Aid also views counselling as too formal an activity. Further, it is seen as an unequal relationship in which the woman counsellor is more powerful, reflecting relationships in society where men are in a more powerful position.

The use of counselling skills by both Home-Start and Women's Aid has been carefully considered in organizational terms. As indicated in Chapter 2, the sensitive, knowledgeable use of counselling skills by project workers is of therapeutic value to the women they work with. Both organizations are clear about boundaries, for them counselling women is inappropriate, and anyone wanting this is referred on. However this is not straightforward. The question of who to refer to is obvious, as there are unlikely to be specialist counselling agencies knowledgeable about domestic violence. One source of stress recognized by Women's Aid workers is frustration arising from relationships with other agency workers where there is a lack of knowledge about the effects of domestic violence. Women's Aid has raised public awareness on this subject, and yet I believe it still remains the organization with a greatest understanding. The workers' dilemma is between maintaining its organizational aims, whilst also recognizing that no other agency can offer what is needed. Some Women's Aid groups surmount this dilemma by initiating, with other women's groups, a local working party to develop counselling services for women subject to violence.

Another response is to organize group counselling since this accords with their ethos, as outlined in Chapter 2.

FEMINIST PERSPECTIVES

In addition to all the variety of theories and techniques used by Feminist counsellors, there are also differences in our Feminist ideology. We don't all need to share the same set of views. Socialist Feminists, radical Feminists, 'green' Feminists and 'spiritual' Feminists can all be successful counsellors, using their Feminism in their counselling to whatever extent they feel comfortable with.

(Chaplin 1988b: 17)

The varieties of Feminism referred to here represent contemporary Feminist thought, known as 'second wave Feminism' (Humm 1992: 53). All point to the central importance of women's experience in formulating any theory. All essentially incorporate an understanding that in all societies which divide the sexes politically, economically and culturally, women are less valued than men. All are optimistic that women can consciously and collectively change their social place.

Of the projects I have explored in this book, Women's Aid, Rape Crisis, and Women's Therapy Centres originated from firm Feminist foundations. The establishment of the first two was heavily influenced by radical Feminist ideas. The latter originated from psychoanalytic Feminism yet remains the place where all types of Feminist counsellors can meet. The remaining projects are influenced by its ideas but in a different sense, in that individual workers adopt a Feminist stance.

A difficulty arises when the Feminist stance is in conflict with the counselling, when they become two discrete ways of operating rather than an integral approach and response. Projects which emphasize the use of counselling skills are less likely to face this dilemma. The earlier example taken from Home-Start, that the value of their work is debatable if it enables a mother to decide to return to work, is perceived as a tension for the organization. However it is embraced as an opportunity to discuss and resolve the implications of a Feminist approach which argues the appropriateness of a mother's right to choose to seek paid employment or not. In a similar way the sensitive use of counselling skills by Women's Aid workers can be incorporated with their aim of 'recognizing a woman as

abused and helping her, if necessary, to recognize herself as abused'
(Scottish Women's Aid 1991: 2).

The difficulty is more apparent in Rape Crisis Centres when radical Feminist ideas cannot be integrated with the counselling models
in use. Many centres can integrate the two theories and the example cited of the Derby centre, where Person-Centred and Gestalt
ideas are informed by radical Feminist theory, is a good illustration.
Yet if the theory becomes a dogma, as in some centres, then the
contrast with the Person-Centred counselling approach emphasizing being with the client where she is, becomes startlingly apparent.
Women seeking help from such centres, who do not find that a
radical Feminist view accords with their own experiences of the
world, have been dismayed when dogma overrules experience. One
client, counselled at a women's project, commented:

> 'when I went to Rape Crisis, it was very much an 'all men are
> bastards' viewpoint. That was no use to me: I didn't believe
> that. My response to the rape felt much more complicated and
> I wanted help in trying to understand it.'

This client was fortunate in finding other counselling resources in
her locality to whom she could turn for help. Others, of course,
may not.

I have referred to the importance and far-reaching significance of
the work of the Women's Therapy Centre writers in the development of psychoanalytic Feminism (Chapters 2 and 3). Additionally,
with the London Women's Therapy Centre being the meeting place
for all types of Feminist counsellors, they are able to contain the
differing views as well as enabling connections to be made and
developed between practitioners.

LIMITATIONS OF COUNSELLING

Great advances have been made by women's counselling projects to
make counselling accessible to women from all walks of life. This
has been a principle which has informed their work from the outset. They are also very aware of the client groups for whom the service does not appear so relevant. Family Centres and Family Service
Units provide services for working class communities yet recognize
that they need to be more proactive in providing counselling for
women from other cultures. Women's Therapy Centres recognize
that they attract fewer clients from certain age groups, namely
women in their late teens and elderly women. It may be that services

need to be offered differently, for instance the setting or timing of the services need re-examining, and how and where they are advertised needs careful consideration. A home visiting counselling service might be appropriate in some situations, or evening appointments may need to be offered. A long-term response is not always appropriate for women in the two under-represented age groups. Young women are at a life stage when they are still changing and maturing quite dramatically and for many a short-term response is more acceptable and age-appropriate. It is worth noting that what an older age group defines as short-term, may be perceived as quite a considerable time by the young.

THE WAY AHEAD

In the 1980s the changes which brought about both the emergence and widespread acceptance of counselling as a rapidly expanding profession, have affected women's projects. Counselling services come to be accepted and expected by women users. One consequence of the growth of training is a body of students seeking to be volunteer counsellors for organizations in exchange for clinical practice and supervision.

The demand for counselling is high and the possibility of providing it by using volunteers becomes increasingly likely. Yet the outlook is bleak for the future of Women's Counselling Projects. In the increasingly difficult economic climate at the time of writing there are indications that many projects will not survive. Counselling services are often the first to be cut when money has to be saved, partly because funders are sceptical about their effectiveness and evaluation procedures. This scepticism fulfils a valuable political role: it is easier to axe services if those responsible can proclaim them to be dubious in nature. Cutting services can then be undertaken in a morally righteous way – the phrase 'saving the tax-payers money' is particularly popular. However such arguments are indeed vacuous when they blatantly ignore, deny, invalidate, or simply fail to seek the opinion of service consumers. At that point these arguments can be seen as rationalizations that act as a cover for dubious government policy. They can be viewed in their true light as the actions of a political structure that does not value women, that does not acknowledge the extent of their suffering and acts in an arbitrary and arrogant fashion. Further, when cost saving, providing long-term services is not seen as justifiable. Such reasoning is ridiculously simplistic and short-sighted, but is nevertheless very powerful. Women's Counselling Projects are extremely vulnerable in such a climate. Funders require quick results, in the name of efficiency, and thereby seek to impose goal orientated counselling. Such an attitude fits well with male-dominated organizations, as outlined in Chapter 5, and uneasily with the projects discussed here. It is an attitude that is remarkable for its ability to glibly use terms such as 'efficiency' and its inability to grasp the real nature of the issues involved. These, of course, face male policy makers with uncomfortable facts – for instance the alarmingly high level of male violence against women.

Many issues which women bring to counselling clearly require a long-term approach. This is partly because of the complexity of these issues affecting so many different levels of her self and life. Women's inner worlds are profoundly affected by their outer world and by their social and political position as well as their history. A longer term approach actively demonstrates to the client that she is of value and accepted for herself, rather than as someone who experiences problems when she occupies a particular role. Clearly, a choice is important. Although for some, short-term work is appropriate, it cannot be a blanket solution. There is a considerable danger of it being used inappropriately as a therapeutic first aid measure, aimed at rapidly repairing a woman's ability to function reasonably in the roles society demands of her. As has been stated previously, women are not a robotic collection of roles, they are to be valued in their own right. In addition, women work differently both reflecting the nature of the work and the essential nature of women. Because this is a move away from traditional male methods, it is not valued by those wishing to save money who do not appreciate this different style, and can be deeply threatened by it. So the way of achieving results, as well as the results themselves, come to be undervalued, misunderstood and not taken seriously. Women are efficient, but they operate and organize differently from men.

If resources are available, in what ways will these projects develop? They show a common desire to be more accessible to certain populations, namely women from different cultures, working class women, and in the case of Women's Therapy Centres, very young and elderly women. One of the elements within second wave Feminism is the black women's movement and theirs is a voice which is increasingly being heard in women's counselling, and this voice needs to be taken seriously.

Other planned developments include the increase in use of volunteer counsellors and the possibility of running counselling groups, both cited as ways of responding to a cutback in resources. Both however require more resources than is immediately obvious. Volunteers require a high level of support if they are not to suffer burn-out, or run the risk of feeling or being exploited. Similarly the preparation for running groups and the level of supervision required is a heavy commitment in time and thought. There are, it seems, no easy answers.

The impact of women's counselling projects in the 1970s and 1980s has been enormous. Their significance is remarkable when it is remembered how few they are in number. Organizations such as Women's Aid and Rape Crisis have had a crucial role in raising public awareness about the nature of violence to women. As a result there are clear indications that this is now taken more seriously, although there is far to go. However the setting up by many police forces of special rape units and domestic violence units is a hopeful sign of progress. The wealth of understanding within these organizations has vastly increased knowledge about the counselling needs of women. This understanding, which is of huge significance evolved from a radical Feminist base: if projects fail to survive then the impact of this theoretical base will be lost, and the ideas will be weakened – they need active expression through practice. Although the ideas will survive at one level, once they become detached from counselling practice and the experience of women working in that particular way they will inevitably be diluted.

Knowledge of women's psychological development, the issues which they bring to counselling, and ways of organizing services run by women for women, all exist within women's counselling projects. The impact they have had, and continue to have, on counselling and psychotherapy is tremendously far-reaching. Whatever happens in terms of financial restraints, women will remain steadfast in coming together to provide services for other women. However, women's commitment to one another, to carry on regardless, should not be exploited by those people – generally men – who are in charge of resource allocation. In many ways and in many areas throughout history women have been used as cheap labour. They have often fulfilled this role apparently willingly, because they believe in what they do, but in reality they have often had little choice. In the writing of this book I have been struck by the care and energy of women at a point when they and their projects are under enormous pressure. It is time that this was taken seriously by those who have the power to ease their path or to block it. Women and women's services are not an optional extra on a male decided menu, and they should not be treated as such. Women and men should have equal power as to how the money is spent.

References

Alban-Metcalf, B. and West, M. (1991) 'Women managers', in Firth-Cozens, J. and West, M. (eds), *Women at Work*. Milton Keynes: Open University Press.

Ashurst, P. and Hall, Z. (1989) *Understanding Women in Distress*. London: Routledge/Tavistock.

Bloch, S. (1977) 'Supportive psychotherapy', *British Journal of Hospital Medicine*, 18(1) July, in Van der Eyken, W. (1982), *Home-Start – A Four Year Evaluation*. Leicester: Home-Start Consultancy.

Bowie, F. and Davies, O. (1990) *Hildegard of Bingham*. London: SPCK.

Braithwaite, W.C. (1961) *The Second Period of Quakerism*, 2nd edn. Cambridge University Press.

British Association for Counselling (1988) *Code of Ethics and Practice for the Supervision of Counsellors*. Rugby: British Association for Counselling.

Brown, G. and Harris, T. (1978) *Social Origins of Depression*. London: Tavistock.

Bryant-Waugh, R. (1991) 'Anorexia Nervosa in boys', in Dolan, B. and Gitzinger, I., *Why Women – Gender Issues and Eating Disorders*. London: European Council on Eating Disorders.

Butler, S. and Wintram, C. (1991) *Feminist Groupwork*. London: Sage.

Carob, A. (1987) *Working with Depressed Women, a Feminist Approach*. London: Gower.

Chaplin, J. (1988a) 'Feminist therapy', in Rowan, J. and Dryden, W. (eds), *Innovative Therapy in Britain*. Milton Keynes: Open University Press.

Chaplin, J. (1988b) *Feminist Counselling in Action*. London: Sage.

Chaplin, J. (1989) 'Counselling and gender', in Dryden, W., Charles-Edwards, D. and Woolfe, R. (eds), *Handbook of Counselling in Britain*. London: Tavistock/Routledge.

Chesler, P. (1972) *Women and Madness*. New York: Doubleday.

Chodorow, N. (1978) *The Reproduction of Mothering*. London: University of California Press.

Derby Rape Crisis (1991) *6th Annual Report*. PO Box 142, Derby.

Dinnerstein, D. (1978) *The Rocking of the Cradle*. London: Souvenir Press.
Dolan, B. and Gitzinger, I. (1991) *Why Women – Gender Issues and Eating Disorders*. London: European Council on Eating Disorders.
Dryden, W. and Thorne, B. (eds) (1991) *Training and Supervision for Counselling in Action*. London: Sage.
Dryden, W., Charles-Edwards, D. and Woolfe, R. (eds) (1989) *Handbook of Counselling in Britain*. London: Tavistock/Routledge.
Egan, G. (1986) *The Skilled Helper*, 3rd edn. Monterey: Brooks/Cole.
Eichenbaum, L. and Orbach, S. (1983) *Understanding Women*. London: Penguin.
Ernst, S. and Goodison, L. (1981) *In our own Hands – A Book of Self-Help Therapy*. London: The Women's Press.
Ernst, S. and Maguire, M. (eds) (1987) *Living with the Sphinx*. London: The Women's Press.
Gillan, P. (1987) *Sex Therapy Manual*. Oxford: Blackwell Scientific Publications.
Gilligan, C. (1982) *In a Different Voice*. Cambridge, MA: Harvard University Press.
Hall, L. and Lloyd, S. (1989) *Surviving Child Sexual Abuse*. London: The Falmer Press.
Hawkins, P. and Shohet, R. (1989) *Supervision in the Helping Professions*. Milton Keynes: Open University Press.
Holdsworth, A. (1988) *Out of the Doll's House*. London: BBC Publications.
Home-Start (1990) 'A gift of time' (notes acccompanying Home-Start video). Leicester: Home-Start Consultancy.
Hooper, D. and Dryden, W. (1991) *Couple Therapy: A Handbook*. Milton Keynes: Open University Press.
Hughes, M. and Kennedy, M. (1985) *New Futures – Changing Women's Education*. London: Routledge and Kegan Paul.
Humm, M. (1992) *Feminisms – A Reader*. Hertford: Harvester Wheatsheaf.
Inskipp, F. and Johns, H. (1984) 'Developmental eclecticism: Egan's skills model of helping', in Dryden, W. (ed.), *Individual Therapy in Britain*. London: Harper and Row.
Jacobs, M. (1986) *The Presenting Past*. Milton Keynes: Open University Press.
Jewett, J. and Haight, E. (1983) 'The emergence of feminine consciousness in supervision', *Journal of Supervision and Training in Ministry*, 6: 164–74.
Kempe, R.S. and Kempe, C. (1978) *Child Abuse*. London: Fontana.
Krzowski, S. and Land, P. (eds) (1988) *In Our Own Experience – Workshops at the Women's Therapy Centre*. London: The Women's Press.
Leicester Relate (1992) *Notes for Prospective Counsellors*. 83 Aylestane Rd, Leicester LE2 7LL.
Mitchell, J. (1975) *Psychoanalysis and Feminism*. London: Penguin.
Nairne, K. and Smith, G. (1984) *Dealing with Depression*. London: The Women's Press.
Oldfield, S. (1983) *The Counselling Relationship*. London: Routledge and Kegan Paul.
Orbach, S. (1978) *Fat is a Feminist Issue*. London: Hamlyn Paperbacks.

Page, F. (1984) 'Gestalt therapy', in Dryden, W. (ed.), *Individual Therapy in Britain*. London: Harper and Row.

Parks, P. (1990) *Rescuing the Inner Child*. London: Condor Books/Souvenir Press.

Perry, J.H. (1989) 'Sexual abuse: is there a process for the counsellor?', *Changes Quarterly*, Summer, 7(3): 93–4.

Perry, J.H. (1992) 'I never go to sleep with my mouth open – working with women sexually abused as children', in Winfield, M. (ed.), *Confronting the Pain of Child Sexual Abuse*. London: Family Service Units.

Plowden, Baroness L. (1967) *Children and their Primary Schools: A Report of the Central Advisory Council for Education, England*. London: Department of Education and Science.

Richman, N. (1976) 'Depression in mothers of pre-school children', *Journal of Child Psychology and Psychiatry*, 17: 75–8.

Rowe, D. (1991) *The Depression Handbook*. London: Collins.

Scottish Women's Aid (1991) *Women Talking To Women – A Women's Aid Approach to Counselling*. Edinburgh: Scottish Women's Aid.

Sturdy, C. (1987) 'Questioning the Sphinx', in Ernst, S. and Maguire, M. (eds), *Living with the Sphinx*. London: The Women's Press.

Thorne, B. (1984) 'Person-centred therapy', in Dryden, W. (ed.), *Individual Therapy in Britain*. London: Harper and Row.

Trevithick, P. (1988) 'Unconsciousness raising with working class women', in Krzowski, S. and Land, P. (eds), *In Our Experience – Workshops at the Women's Therapy Centre*. London: The Women's Press.

Van der Eyken, W. (1982) *Home-Start – A Four Year Evaluation*. Leicester: Home-Start Consultancy.

Walker, M. (1990) *Women in Therapy and Counselling*. Milton Keynes: Open University Press.

Walker, M. (1992) *Surviving Secrets*. Buckingham: Open University Press.

Wallis, M. (1992) *Women Hold Up More Than Half The Sky*. Northampton: Pen Green Centre Publications. (MEd thesis, University of Leicester.)

What is Women's Aid? (1992) Leaflet. Bristol: Women's Aid Federation, England.

Woodward, J. (1988) *Understanding Ourselves – The Uses of Therapy*. Basingstoke: Macmillan Education.

Wyatt, G.E. and Powell, G.J. (1988) *Lasting Effects of Child Sexual Abuse*. London: Sage.

Index